Crystallization-Study
of
Genesis

Volume Six

Witness Lee

The Holy Word for Morning Revival

Living Stream Ministry
Anaheim, CA • www.lsm.org

© 2014 Living Stream Ministry

First Edition, August 2014.

ISBN 978-0-7363-7080-6

Published by

Living Stream Ministry
2431 W. La Palma Ave., Anaheim, CA 92801 U.S.A.
P. O. Box 2121, Anaheim, CA 92814 U.S.A.

Printed in the United States of America

14 15 16 17 / 5 4 3 2 1

2014 Summer Training

CRYSTALLIZATION-STUDY
OF GENESIS

Contents

Preface

1. This book is intended as an aid to believers in developing a daily time of morning revival with the Lord in His word. At the same time, it provides a limited review of the summer training held June 30—July 5, 2014, in Anaheim, California, on the continuation of the "Crystallization-study of Genesis." Through intimate contact with the Lord in His word, the believers can be constituted with life and truth and thereby equipped to prophesy in the meetings of the church unto the building up of the Body of Christ.

2. The book is divided into weeks. One training message is covered per week. Each week presents first the message outline, followed by six daily portions, a hymn, and then some space for writing. The training outline has been divided into days, corresponding to the six daily portions. Each daily portion covers certain points and begins with a section entitled "Morning Nourishment." This section contains selected verses and a short reading that can provide rich spiritual nourishment through intimate fellowship with the Lord. The "Morning Nourishment" is followed by a section entitled "Today's Reading," a longer portion of ministry related to the day's main points. Each day's portion concludes with a short list of references for further reading and some space for the saints to make notes concerning their spiritual inspiration, enlightenment, and enjoyment to serve as a reminder of what they have received of the Lord that day.

3. The space provided at the end of each week is for composing a short prophecy. This prophecy can be composed by considering all of our daily notes, the "harvest" of our inspirations during the week, and preparing a main point with some sub-points to be spoken in the church meetings for the organic building up of the Body of Christ.

4. Following the last week in this volume, we have provided reading schedules for both the Old and New Testaments in the Recovery Version with footnotes. These schedules are arranged so that one can read through both the Old and

New Testaments of the Recovery Version with footnotes in two years.

5. As a practical aid to the saints' feeding on the Word throughout the day, we have provided verse cards at the end of the volume, which correspond to each day's Scripture reading. These may be cut out and carried along as a source of spiritual enlightenment and nourishment in the saints' daily lives.

6. The content of this book is taken primarily from *Crystallization-study Outlines: Genesis (3),* the text and footnotes of the Recovery Version of the Bible, selections from the writings of Witness Lee and Watchman Nee, and *Hymns,* all of which are published by Living Stream Ministry.

7. *Crystallization-study Outlines: Genesis (3)* was compiled by Living Stream Ministry from the writings of Witness Lee and Watchman Nee. The outlines, footnotes, and cross-references in the Recovery Version of the Bible are by Witness Lee. Unless otherwise noted, the references cited in this publication are by Witness Lee.

8. For the sake of space, references to *The Collected Works of Watchman Nee* and *The Collected Works of Witness Lee* are abbreviated to *CWWN* and *CWWL,* respectively.

Summer Training
(June 30—July 5, 2014)

CRYSTALLIZATION-STUDY
OF GENESIS

Banners:

Jacob's dream was a dream of God's goal,
the dream of Bethel,
the dream of the house of God,
which is the church today and
which will consummate in the New Jerusalem
as the eternal dwelling place of God
and His redeemed elect.

After we experience the breaking
of our natural life
and undergo transformation for God's building,
we will make a crucial and radical turn
from the individual experience of God
to the corporate experience of God—
the experience of God as the God of Bethel.

When Jacob prophesied
concerning his twelve sons with blessing,
he was a God-man,
a man filled, constituted, permeated,
and even reorganized with God;
whatever he thought was God's thought,
and whatever opinion he expressed
was God's opinion.

God's intention in creating man in His image
and in giving him dominion
was that man would become a reproduction
of God for His corporate expression
and would exercise God's authority
to deal with the enemy, recover the earth,
and bring in the kingdom.

The Life of Joseph
as a Copy of the Life of Christ
and
Living as a Sheaf of Life
and as a Star of Light

Scripture Reading: Gen. 37:2, 5-11, 19; 41:40-46

Day 1 I. **Joseph's life was a copy of the life of Christ in the following aspects:**
   A. In his being a shepherd (Gen. 37:2; John 10:11-16).
   B. In his being his father's beloved (Gen. 37:3-4; Matt. 3:17; 17:5).
   C. In his being sent by his father to minister to his brothers according to his father's will (Gen. 37:12-17; John 6:38).
   D. In his being hated, persecuted, and betrayed (sold) by his brothers (Gen. 37:5, 18-36; John 15:25; Matt. 26:4, 14-16).
Day 2 E. In his being cast into the prison of death with two criminals, one of whom was restored, and the other, executed (Gen. 39:20; 40:1-23; Acts 2:23; Luke 23:32, 39-43).
   F. In his being released (resurrected) from the prison of death (Gen. 41:14; Acts 2:24).
   G. In his being enthroned with authority (Gen. 41:40-44; Matt. 28:18; Acts 2:36; Rev. 3:21).
   H. In his receiving glory and gifts (Gen. 41:42; Heb. 2:9; Psa. 68:18; Acts 2:33).
   I. In his becoming the savior of the world, the sustainer of life (the revealer of secrets) (Gen. 41:45; Acts 5:31; John 6:50-51):
      1. First, Joseph was the revealer of secrets (Gen. 40:9-19; 41:17-32).
      2. Then, because he sustained the life of the people (vv. 47-57; 47:12-24), he became the savior of the world (v. 25).

J. In his taking a wife from the Gentiles (41:45; John 3:29; Eph. 5:23-27; Rev. 19:7).

K. In his supplying people with food (Gen. 41:56-57; John 6:35).

L. In his acknowledging his ignorant brothers and being recognized by them (Gen. 45:1-4, 14-15; Rom. 11:26; Zech. 12:10; Rev. 1:7).

M. In his reigning in the kingdom over the whole earth (Gen. 41:40—50:26; Rev. 11:15; Dan. 7:13-14).

Day 3 II. **Joseph, a "master of dreams" (Gen. 37:19), dreamed that according to God's view, His people are sheaves of wheat full of life and heavenly bodies full of light (vv. 5-11):**

A. Joseph's two dreams (vv. 7-9), both from God, unveiled to him God's divine view concerning the nature, position, function, and goal of God's people on earth:

1. In his first dream Joseph saw sheaves in the field bowing down to his sheaf; this dream reveals that, at the most, Joseph was just a sheaf and that, at the worst, his brothers were also sheaves; Joseph was a sheaf, and his brothers were sheaves (vv. 7-8):

   a. The only difference between him and them was that God had chosen him to reign, but this does not mean that he was better than they were; God's people are all sheaves of life in Christ.

   b. God spoke through Balaam, and Balaam said, "He has not beheld iniquity in Jacob, / Nor has He seen trouble in Israel" (Num. 23:21a):

      (1) This word was spoken not according to the human view but according to the divine view; in the sight of God, Israel is without fault.

      (2) In themselves God's people have many defects, but in God's redemption and in Christ they have no defects; when

God looks at His people, He does not see them according to what they are in themselves but according to what they are in Christ (cf. 2 Cor. 5:16-17).

c. Elijah complained against Israel, saying, "The children of Israel have forsaken Your covenant, thrown down Your altars, and slain Your prophets with the sword; and I alone am left, and they seek to take my life"; however, Jehovah replied, "Yet I have left Myself seven thousand in Israel, all the knees that have not bowed unto Baal and every mouth that has not kissed him" (1 Kings 19:10, 18; cf. Rom. 11:2-5).

d. If we have seen the heavenly dream, then we have seen that in God's view all His people are sheaves full of life to produce food for the meal offering to satisfy God and man (Lev. 2:4-5).

Day 4

2. In his second dream Joseph saw the sun, the moon, and eleven stars bowing down to him (Gen. 37:9):

a. According to their fallen nature, God's people are evil and unclean, but in God's eternal view, His people are heavenly bodies full of light (cf. Rev. 12:1 and footnote).

b. The reigning aspect of the mature life never condemns God's people; rather, it shepherds and appreciates them (Gen. 37:5-11; cf. 1 Cor. 13:4-8, 13).

c. One thing is certain: whoever condemns the church or blames the saints will suffer the loss of life; however, if we praise the Lord for His saints being full of life and light, we will be the first to participate in life (Gen. 12:2-3; Num. 24:9).

B. Although God's people are positioned in heaven as the sun, the moon, and the stars, they are living on earth as sheaves (Phil. 3:20; 2:15), for sheaves grow in the field; today we are the heavenly people living on earth.

C. We have to use the "divine telescope" to see through time and behold the New Jerusalem, where there is nothing but sheaves full of life and stars full of light.

Day 5

D. Although the sons of Jacob were sinful, Christ still came in through them (Gen. 38:27-30; Matt. 1:3).

E. The more mature in life we become, the less we will speak negatively concerning the saints or the church; we are not the ones to judge (7:1-5; Rom. 14:4).

III. **Joseph's dreams controlled his life and directed his behavior (cf. Acts 26:19):**

A. Joseph behaved so excellently and marvelously because he was directed by the vision that he saw in his dreams.

B. Joseph lived a life that corresponded to the vision he saw in his two dreams; his brothers vented their anger (Gen. 37:18-31) and indulged in their lust (38:15-18), but Joseph subdued his anger and conquered his lust (39:7-23), behaving as a sheaf full of life and conducting himself like a heavenly star shining in the darkness:

Day 6

1. While Joseph's brothers were drowning in the water of human anger, Joseph, representing the reigning aspect of a mature life, lived as a sheaf of life and emerged from the death water of human anger (37:18).

2. Judah behaved in a blind way, indulging in his lust in darkness (38:15-18); in contrast, Joseph, living as a star of light, overcame his lust (39:7-12).

C. Joseph's life under the heavenly vision was the life of the kingdom of the heavens described in Matthew 5—7; by living such a life, he was fully prepared to reign as a king; according to the constitution of the heavenly kingdom revealed in these chapters in Matthew, our anger must be subdued, and our lust must be conquered (5:21-32).

D. As the kingdom people in the kingdom life, we are being trained to be kings, to be Josephs, to manifest the reigning aspect of the mature life.

Morning Nourishment

Gen. ...Joseph, when he was seventeen years old, was
37:2-4 shepherding the flock with his brothers while he
was *still* a youth....Now Israel loved Joseph more
than all his sons because he was the son of his old
age, and he had made him a coat of many colors.
And when his brothers saw that their father loved
him more than all his brothers, they hated him and
could not speak peaceably to him.

Joseph is the perfect type of Christ because he portrays the
constituted aspect of a mature saint. If the aspect of you which
is constituted of Christ is not perfect, then surely no part of you
could be perfect. In us who are fallen, saved, called, redeemed,
and regenerated there is nothing perfect except the constituting
Christ. Hallelujah, we have Christ's constitution within us!...
This aspect, Christ constituted in the matured saints, is perfect.
Hence, it perfectly typifies Christ. (*Life-study of Genesis,* p. 1410)

Today's Reading

Joseph, like Abel, was a shepherd (Gen. 37:2). This typifies
the aspect of the constitution of Christ in the mature life that
is the shepherding life to take care of others. In chapter 37
Joseph not only fed and shepherded the flock;...he was sent
by his father to [also] shepherd his brothers. Thus, Joseph
shepherded not only his father's flock, but also his father's
sons. The Lord Jesus also came as a shepherd (John 10:11).

The reigning aspect is firstly the shepherding aspect. If
you do not have the burden to shepherd others and to feed
them, you will never be able to reign. Reigning authority comes
from the shepherding life. Eventually, Joseph reigned over his
brothers. But he did not reign over them until he had already
shepherded them. He was sent by his father to shepherd his
brothers and to feed them. In like manner, Jesus came not as a
King to rule others; He came as a Shepherd.

As the Shepherd, Christ was killed by His own people. This is
revealed in John 10, where we are told that the good Shepherd

gives His life for the sheep. Jesus came as the Shepherd and was killed, giving His life for His flock. In principle, the same thing happened to Joseph in Genesis 37. Although he was sent to shepherd his brothers, they nearly killed him. Joseph gave his life in order to carry out this kind of shepherding. It is good that we have a shepherding life within. But if you are to shepherd others, you must be ready to be killed by those you are caring for.

Joseph, the one with the shepherding aspect, was also his father's beloved (37:3-4). Likewise, Christ was the Father's beloved Son (Matt. 3:17; 17:5). Only that aspect of us that is constituted of Christ is beloved in the eyes of God....This part of us is beloved of the Father....You have had the deep sense that God the Father was present. Whenever you have this sense, it is a proof that you have the constitution of Christ, which is pleasing to the Father. Of that part of your being the Father will always say, "This is My beloved."

In Genesis 37:12-17 we see that Joseph ministered to the brothers according to his father's will. In this matter also Joseph was a type of Christ, for Christ came down from heaven to do the will of the One who had sent Him (John 6:38).

If you read this section of the Word, you will admit not only that Joseph was a type of Christ, but that his biography is virtually the biography of Christ. Joseph's life was a copy of Christ's.

Although Joseph was a shepherd and the father's beloved and although he ministered to his brothers according to his father's will, he was hated and harassed by the brothers to whom he ministered (Gen. 37:4-5, 8, 11, 18-36). The same was true of Christ (Acts 10:38-39). Christ was sent to minister to the children of God, but they hated Him. According to the Gospels, the Jewish leaders hated Christ, conspired against Him, and plotted to kill Him. This was also Joseph's experience with his brothers. In Genesis 37:19 and 20 his brothers said, "Here comes this master of dreams. Now then, come and let us slay him...." Thus, they conspired and plotted against their brother Joseph. (*Life-study of Genesis,* pp. 1410-1413)

Further Reading: Life-study of Genesis, msg. 110

Enlightenment and inspiration: _____

_____

_____

_____

Morning Nourishment

Gen. **And Pharaoh was angry with his two officials, the**
40:2-3 **chief of the cupbearers and the chief of the bakers.**
And he put them in custody at the house of the cap-
tain of the guard, in the prison, the place where
Joseph was confined.

Joseph's betrayal was followed by a period of confinement, a period of imprisonment (Gen. 39:20). Joseph was with two criminals, who typified the two criminals with Christ, one of whom was restored and the other executed (40:1-23). It was the same with Christ. After Christ was betrayed, He was put into the prison of death (Acts 2:23). He was crucified between two criminals, one of whom was saved and the other perished (Luke 23:32, 39-43). Christ was confined in the prison of death for three days and three nights. As a type of Christ, Joseph had the same experience as Christ. He was rejected by his brothers, sold by them, and eventually cast into prison. Christ suffered the same things. (*Life-study of Genesis,* pp. 1433-1434)

Today's Reading

Joseph typified Christ as the One resurrected from the prison of death (Gen. 41:14; Acts 2:24). Christ was not arrested and cast into prison. Rather, He walked willingly into prison, that is, He went into the prison of death voluntarily. Although He entered into death willingly, the gates of Hades, which is the power of death, the authority of darkness, immediately rose up and sought to keep Him there forever. But as Acts 2:24 says, it was impossible for Him to be held by death....Christ could not be held by death because He is resurrection (John 11:25)....Resurrection is definitely more powerful than death....Therefore, Christ walked out of death. To Him, this walking out of death was His resurrection. As Joseph was released from the dungeon, so Christ was also released from the prison of death.

Joseph also typified Christ as the One enthroned with authority (Gen. 41:40-44; Matt. 28:18; Acts 2:36; Rev. 3:21). On the same day Joseph was released from the dungeon, he was enthroned to be the actual ruler over the whole land of Egypt. In like manner, after Christ was resurrected, He was enthroned with authority. Acts 2:36 says that the crucified and resurrected Christ has been made both Lord and Christ.... This refers to Christ's enthronement.

When Christ was enthroned, He received glory (Heb. 2:9). Joseph also typifies Christ in this regard, for when he was released from the dungeon, he received glory (Gen. 41:42). Joseph's opposers not only sold him and despised him, but cast him into a dungeon. In chapter 41 the prison is called a dungeon. The living conditions in Joseph's dungeon were far worse than the conditions of the prisons in this country today. The dungeon into which Joseph was cast was a pit. Those who put him there did so with the intention that he would be severely distressed. But God lifted him up and not only placed him on the throne but also gave him glory. You may be wondering how we can prove that Joseph received glory. The proof is in the fact that he was clothed with beautiful garments and made to ride in the second chariot of Pharaoh (41:42-43). His being clothed with fine linen was in contrast with his being stripped by his brothers of his coat of many colors (37:23). When people saw him clothed with such beautiful garments and sitting in Pharaoh's chariot, they must have realized that here was a man in glory.

When Joseph was released from the dungeon and uplifted to the throne, he received gifts (41:42). Christ also has received gifts (Acts 2:33). Many Christians know that Christ resurrected, ascended, and has been crowned with honor and glory, but not many know that after Christ's ascension, enthronement, and glorification He also received gifts. Acts 2:33 says that Christ received of the Father the promise of the Holy Spirit, which He has poured out. What Christ received of the Father was a gift. In ancient times, many centuries before Christ, the same thing happened to Joseph. Joseph was not only glorified but also received gifts. (*Life-study of Genesis,* pp. 1445-1447)

Further Reading: Life-study of Genesis, msgs. 112-113

Enlightenment and inspiration: _____

_____

_____

_____

Morning Nourishment

Gen. Then Joseph had a dream; and when he told *it* to
37:5 his brothers, they hated him even more.
   7 There we were, binding sheaves in the field, when
      suddenly my sheaf rose up and remained stand-
      ing; and then your sheaves gathered around and
      bowed down to my sheaf.

If you had been Joseph, would you have considered your brothers heavenly and full of life and light? In Genesis 37:2 we are told
that Joseph brought to his father an evil report regarding his
brothers. Furthermore, according to chapter 37, Joseph's brothers
were full of hatred and anger, and according to chapter 38, they
were full of lust. In chapter 37 we see the hatred and anger of
Joseph's brothers, and in chapter 38 we see Judah's lust. Joseph
saw the evil of his brothers and reported it to his father. But
Joseph had two dreams (37:5-9). In the first dream Joseph saw
sheaves in the field. This dream reveals that, at the most, Joseph
was just a sheaf and that, at the worst, his brothers also were
sheaves. God gave Joseph this dream, and in it he had God's view
of his brothers....God came to give Joseph a dream, and He
seemed to say, "Joseph, in My eyes you are the same as your
brothers, and they are just as good as you are. You are a sheaf, and
they also are sheaves. The only difference between you and them
is that I have chosen you to reign. But this does not mean that you
are better than they are." (*Life-study of Genesis*, pp. 1414-1415)

Today's Reading

If we do not have experience, we shall not be able to understand the word in the Bible regarding Joseph's dream of the
sheaves....The more you love the church and care for the saints,
the more "gophers," "turtles," and "scorpions" you will see. Then
you will say, "Lord, what is this? Lord, the situation in the church
is pitiful. Not even the elders are any good. And look at all the
sisters! I don't want to sit near them in the meetings." At such a
time you need a heavenly dream. When the dream comes, the

Lord will tell you, "You are not any better, and the others are not worse than you. You are all sheaves of life in Me. There are no 'gophers,' 'scorpions,' or 'turtles' among My people. All are sheaves full of life." If I had not seen such a heavenly dream, I would have quit long ago. But I have seen the dream. I have seen that I am a sheaf and that all those who in my eyes are "gophers" are sheaves also. In the eyes of God, they are sheaves.

Years ago, I prayed many accusing prayers to the Lord; I reported to Him the evils I had seen....But the Lord said, "I don't look at them from your view. I see them from My view. In the New Jerusalem there are no 'gophers' and 'scorpions.'"

According to the book of Numbers, the children of Israel had done many evil things. Balaam was hired by a heathen king to curse Israel and to expose the evil in Israel. But God spoke through Balaam, and Balaam said, "He has not beheld iniquity in Jacob, / Nor has He seen trouble in Israel" (Num. 23:21). God seemed to be saying, "I have not beheld any iniquity in My people. I do not see any perverseness in them."

Elijah complained against Israel saying, "The children of Israel have forsaken Your covenant, thrown down Your altars, and slain Your prophets with the sword; and I alone am left, and they seek to take my life" (1 Kings 19:10). Elijah was accusing Israel before God. Being displeased with this, the Lord replied, "I have left Myself seven thousand in Israel, all the knees that have not bowed unto Baal and every mouth that has not kissed him" (1 Kings 19:18). Do not go to the Lord in the way of accusing others before Him. Instead, you should say to Him, "Lord, since You see no iniquity, I do not choose to see any either. All the 'gophers' and 'scorpions' are sheaves, and I love them."...If you have seen the heavenly dream, then you have seen that in God's view all His people are sheaves full of life to produce food for the meal offering to satisfy God and man. (*Life-study of Genesis,* pp. 1415-1416)

Further Reading: Life-study of Genesis, msgs. 115, 118

Enlightenment and inspiration: _____

_____

_____

_____

Morning Nourishment

Gen. And he had still another dream and told it to his
37:9 brothers and said, Now I have had another dream:
There were the sun and the moon and eleven stars,
bowing down to me.

Rev. And a great sign was seen in heaven: a woman
12:1 clothed with the sun, and the moon underneath
her feet, and on her head a crown of twelve stars.

In the Bible there is the principle of confirmation by two witnesses. Thus, Joseph had two dreams. In Joseph's second dream he saw the sun, the moon, and the eleven stars bowing down to him (Gen. 37:9). This indicates that in the eyes of God all the condemned and accused people are full of light. Be careful not to accuse the brothers and sisters. The reigning aspect of the maturity of life never condemns others. Rather, it shepherds and appreciates them. It says, "Oh, the church life and all the saints are wonderful! The saints are sheaves full of life. How nourishing and satisfying they are! Furthermore, they are heavenly luminaries full of light." If you say that it is a lie to speak this way and that you cannot do it, it means that you have not seen the dream, the vision. You are lacking the heavenly view. (*Life-study of Genesis*, pp. 1416-1417)

Today's Reading

Perhaps some years ago you felt positively about all the brothers and sisters, but not today....Today you need the view of the heavenly dream. In Genesis 37 there are two dreams. One is of sheaves full of life, and the other of the heavenly host full of light. This is God's view, the heavenly view, of His people. Because I have this heavenly view, I am greatly encouraged. I am not working with "gophers" and "scorpions." I am serving the sheaves, I am under the sun and moon, and I am walking among the stars. The dream Joseph saw is similar to the vision in Revelation 12, where God's people are signified by the woman clothed with the sun, with the moon under her feet, and with the crown of twelve stars upon her head. We need such a vision to see God's people from the heavenly viewpoint.

One thing is certain: Whoever condemns the church or blames the saints will suffer the loss of life. There is not one exception to this. You may be right, and the church may actually be wrong. The condition of the saints may be that of "gophers" and "scorpions." But if you condemn them, you will suffer the loss of life. However, if you say, "Lord, I praise You because Your people are full of life and light," you will be the first to participate in life. For this reason, I dare not say that the brothers and sisters are not good. Rather, I always say, "Praise the Lord! How good the saints are!" When I do this, I enjoy life. But if I were to criticize the brothers and sisters, I would immediately suffer death. No one who speaks negatively concerning the church or the saints enjoys life. On the contrary, all those who speak negatively suffer death. We need to say, "Praise the Lord, my brother will be a heavenly light! If he is not so today, he will be in the future." With God there is no time element. There is no clock in heaven, only eternity. As God views His people from the standpoint of eternity, He sees them all as sheaves full of life and as the sun, moon, and stars full of light.

Although God's people are positioned in heaven as the sun, the moon, and the stars, they are living on earth as sheaves (Phil. 3:20; 2:15), for sheaves grow in the field. Today we are the heavenly people living on earth.

We are God's people. I have been encouraged, strengthened, and edified by this. I have complete faith in you all, and I expect to see you all in the New Jerusalem. I like to have an eternal view, not the view from the earth....If you use the "divine telescope" to see through time, you will behold the New Jerusalem where there is nothing but sheaves and stars. In the New Jerusalem there are no "gophers" or "scorpions." There, everything is full of life and light. When we consider Joseph's dreams, we realize that no human mind could have conceived the book of Genesis. Only God could have caused Joseph to have these dreams. (*Life-study of Genesis,* pp. 1417-1418)

Further Reading: Life-study of Genesis, msg. 120

Enlightenment and inspiration: _____

_____

_____

_____

Morning Nourishment

Matt. And Judah begot Pharez and Zarah of Tamar, and
1:3   Pharez begot Hezron, and Hezron begot Aram.
7:1   Do not judge, that you be not judged.

Although the sons of Jacob were sinful, Christ still came
through them (Gen. 38:27-30; Matt. 1:3). Out of the gross sin committed in Genesis 38, two sons were born, the first of whom was a
forefather of Christ. Pharez, mentioned in the genealogy of Christ
in Matthew 1, was one of Christ's forefathers. According to the holy
word of Scripture, Christ came through the sinful sons of Jacob.
It is similar to David's sin with Bathsheba. The issue of that sin
was Solomon, who was also a forefather of Christ, one through
whom Christ came (Matt. 1:6). (*Life-study of Genesis,* p. 1419)

Today's Reading

The mature life has a reigning aspect. The more mature in
life you become, the less you will speak negatively concerning
the saints or the church. When we came into the church, we had
a church-life honeymoon. The honeymoon, however, never lasts
very long....But one day the heavenly dream will come, and your
view will be revolutionized. You will realize that you dare not
say anything negative concerning the church or the saints. On
the contrary, you will say, "This is the church, and this is God's
people. In God's eyes the believers are all sheaves. They are also
the sun, the moon, and the stars." When you come to this stage,
you will not dare to say anything negative about the church.

After seeing such a vision, I have nevertheless said at times,
"Yes, I have seen that the church is wonderful. But actually it is
not so." In saying this, the "tail" was exposed...[and] caused me to
suffer death. Eventually, I was completely subdued and convinced,
and I said, "Lord, I forget my short sight and use the divine telescope. The church is excellent, marvelous, and wonderful. There is
nothing wrong with the church. It is perfect and complete." When
I speak like this, I am full of life and I enjoy life. To me, every
brother and sister is wonderful, and I love them all, including the
backsliders. The more I speak this way about the brothers and

sisters, the more I am full of life. I believe many of us have experienced this. We are not the ones to judge. God is the Judge. And He is not judging the saints; He is working on them to transform the "scorpions" into sheaves and the "gophers" into stars. Eventually, we all shall be sheaves and stars. May we all have this eternal view.

Joseph behaved so excellently and marvelously because he was directed by the vision he saw in his dreams....If even the little ones are influenced by what they see [on television], then how much more was the young man Joseph influenced by the heavenly vision, the vision that he was a sheaf rising up full of life and that he was a star worshipped by all the other stars!... Joseph's excellent and marvelous behavior was due to the vision he received. The vision of his two dreams controlled his life and directed his behavior. He behaved as the sheaf standing up and full of life, and he conducted himself like a heavenly star shining in the darkness.

In [Genesis 37 through 38] two gross sins are recorded. In chapter 37 there is the sin of anger (37:18-28). Joseph's brothers seized the opportunity to give full vent to their anger. This was not an insignificant case of anger. The one Joseph's brothers were plotting to kill was not a thief, but their own brother in the flesh, the dear son of their own father. If they had had any human affection at all, they would never have considered doing such a thing. Reuben, however, did think of how it would affect their father; and Judah suggested that they not kill him, but sell him, which was far superior to shedding his blood. Nevertheless, in chapter 37 we see the anger of Joseph's brothers. In the next chapter, chapter 38, we have Judah's indulgence in lust, even in incest (38:15-18). After the fall of man, the first issue to come forth was the killing of a brother in the flesh. And the sin that brought in the flood as God's judgment upon the fallen race was the indulgence in lust. These two sins, the sins of murdering a brother in the flesh and of indulging in lust, are repeated here. (*Life-study of Genesis,* pp. 1419-1420, 1424-1425)

Further Reading: Life-study of Exodus, msg. 7

Enlightenment and inspiration: _____

_____
_____
_____

Morning Nourishment

Matt. But I say to you that everyone who is angry with
5:22 his brother shall be liable to the judgment...

Gen. There is no one greater in this house than I, and he
39:9 has withheld nothing from me except you, because
you are his wife. How then can I do this great evil,
and sin against God?

12 ...[Joseph] left his garment in her hand, and fled
and went outside.

The anger of his brothers afforded Joseph the opportunity to live as a sheaf of life. While all his brothers were drowning in the water of anger, Joseph, the reigning aspect of the mature life, lived as a sheaf of life, emerging from the death water of human anger. The record, under God's inspiration, uses fallen anger as the background to demonstrate how much life was in the sheaf. This sheaf was filled with life. When all the rest had sunk into the death water of human anger, this sheaf emerged and survived in that situation of death. (*Life-study of Genesis,* pp. 1425-1426)

Today's Reading

The second gross sin, the indulgence in lust, also afforded Joseph an opportunity. The indulgence in lust seen in Genesis chapter 38 is a symbol of darkness. In this chapter Judah was utterly in darkness. Judah behaved in a blind way, and blindness signifies darkness. If he had not been in blindness, in darkness, how could he have committed adultery with his daughter-in-law? Where was his conscience? Where was his eyesight? His eyes had been blackened and blinded, and he was in darkness. That evil woman in chapter 39, the wife of Potiphar, was also in darkness. If she had not been in darkness, how could she have behaved in such an evil way? Thus, in chapters 38 and 39 we have a portrait of darkness.

But in the midst of this darkness we see Joseph as a bright star shining in the heavens (39:7-12). Conducting himself as a shining star, Joseph seemed to be saying, "All you people are under darkness, but I am shining upon you. How can I, a bright star, do such a dark thing? I cannot forget my dream. My dream controls me and directs me. As a heavenly star, I would never sell my position." If you have this light as you come to these chapters, you will see that Joseph was one who lived a life that corresponded to his vision. Joseph was not only a dreamer; he was also one who practiced, one who lived out, what he saw in his dream.

Just as we all have anger, we also have lust. If you have no lust, then you must be a bench or a stone. Every human being has lust. The way to control our lust is to be subdued, controlled, and directed by the vision.

The function of the vision is similar to that of brakes in a car. In times of danger, we step on the brakes. The vision of the heavenly star is a powerful brake for our spiritual car.

Joseph's life under the heavenly vision was the life of the kingdom of the heavens described in Matthew 5, 6, and 7. According to the constitution of the heavenly kingdom revealed in these chapters in Matthew, our anger must be subdued and our lust conquered (Matt. 5:21-32). If we claim to be the kingdom people, yet we cannot subdue our anger or conquer our lust, we are finished. Instead of being in the kingdom, we are on the seashore. We are those giving vent to our anger and indulging in lust. But all the kingdom people subdue their anger and conquer their lust. This is the kingdom life.

In the kingdom life today, kings are being trained. We, the kingdom people in the kingdom life, are being trained to be kings, to be Josephs, to be the reigning aspect of the mature life. For this, we must subdue our anger and conquer our lust. What a wonderful picture Joseph's life is of our experience today! Day by day, we are subduing our anger and conquering our lust. Instead of agreeing with our anger or cooperating with our lust, we reject our anger and condemn our lust, because we are the reigning aspect of the mature life. We have the constitution of Christ within us, and we are being prepared to reign as kings. (*Life-study of Genesis*, pp. 1426-1429)

Further Reading: Life-study of Genesis, msg. 111

Enlightenment and inspiration: _____

_____
_____
_____

Hymns, #947

1   God's Kingdom today is a real exercise,
But when Christ comes to reign it will be a great prize;
It is wisdom divine that we now may be trained
That His plan be fulfilled and His justice maintained.

2   God's children, we're born to be kings with His Son,
And we need to be trained that we may overcome
And to know how to rule in His kingdom as kings,
That His kingship thru us be expressed o'er all things.

3   Today we must learn to submit to His throne,
How to have a strict life and His government own;
His authority then we'll be able to share,
O'er the nations to rule with God's Son as the heir.

4   With a life strict to self we must righteousness hold,
Kind to others in peace, and with God joyful, bold;
In the Kingdom's reality e'er to remain,
For its manifestation prepared thus to reign.

5   Then Christ when He comes with the kingdom from God
Will to us grant His kingship to share as reward;
Thus the Lord will His righteousness thru us maintain
And His wisdom to heavenly powers make plain.

6   For this the Apostle pressed on at all cost,
For the Kingdom assured that he would not be lost;
'Tis for this he charged others, Be true to the Lord,
That the Kingdom might be unto them a reward.

7   O Lord, give us grace for Thy Kingdom to live,
To be trained that Thou may the reward to us give;
Make the Kingdom's reality our exercise,
That its manifestation may be our great prize.

Composition for prophecy with main point and sub-points: _____

_____
_____
_____
_____
_____
_____
_____
_____
_____
_____
_____
_____
_____
_____
_____
_____
_____
_____
_____
_____
_____
_____
_____
_____
_____
_____
_____
_____
_____
_____
_____
_____
_____
_____
_____

Joseph—the Reigning Aspect
of the Mature Life

Scripture Reading: Gen. 41:39-44, 51-52; 45:5-8; 47:14-23; 50:15-21

Day 1   I. According to spiritual experience, Jacob and Joseph are one person; Joseph represents the reigning aspect of the mature Israel, the constitution of Christ in Jacob's mature nature; as a mature saint constituted of Christ, the perfect One, Jacob reigned through Joseph (Gen. 41:39-44; Heb. 6:1a; Gal. 6:8; 5:22-23):

A. The reigning aspect typified by Joseph is Christ constituted into our being (4:19).

B. The reigning aspect of the mature life is a life that always enjoys the presence of the Lord; wherever His presence is, there is authority, the ruling power (Gen. 39:2-5, 21-23):

1. In the presence of the Lord, Joseph was prospered by Him (vv. 2-3, 23); while Joseph was undergoing ill-treatment, he enjoyed the Lord's prosperity that came to him under the Lord's sovereignty.

2. In the presence of the Lord, Joseph was favored with the Lord's blessing wherever he was; when Joseph enjoyed prosperity, he and those who were involved with him were blessed (vv. 4-5, 22-23).

Day 2   C. Although his own dreams were not yet fulfilled, Joseph had the faith and the boldness to interpret the dreams of his two companions in prison (40:8); eventually, Joseph was released from prison indirectly through his speaking by faith in interpreting the cupbearer's dream (41:9-13), and he was ushered to the throne directly through his speaking boldly in interpreting Pharaoh's dreams (vv. 14-46); both release and authority came to him through his speaking:

1. Andrew Murray once said a word like this: the good minister of the Word should always minister more than he has experienced; this means that we should speak more according to the vision than according to the fulfillment of the vision.

2. Even if our vision has not been fulfilled, we should still speak of it to others; the time will come when our vision will be fulfilled; Joseph's dreams were eventually fulfilled through his interpretation of the dream of the cupbearer.

Day 3

3. If we are living out Christ, we will bring either life or death wherever we are (2 Cor. 2:14-16); to the cupbearer, Joseph brought restoration; to the baker, he brought execution (Gen. 41:12-13).

D. If we seek the Lord, He will put us into a "dungeon"; without the dungeon we cannot ascend to the throne; we must not be a dungeon dropout; we must stay in the dungeon until we graduate and receive the crown (James 1:12; cf. Phil. 3:8).

E. We should not speak according to our feelings but according to the heavenly vision; we are visionaries, seers, of God's eternal economy, so we should speak according to the absoluteness of the truth of His economy (Acts 26:16-19):

1. The visions that Joseph saw not only controlled his life but also sustained his faith.

2. Because Joseph was important and valuable, the time of his testing could not be shortened.

Day 4

F. In his receiving glory and gifts in his enthronement, Joseph typifies Christ, who received glory (Heb. 2:9) and gifts (Psa. 68:18; Acts 2:33) in His ascension (Gen. 41:42):

1. The ring, the garments, and the gold chain portray the gifts that Christ received in His

ascension to the heavens, which gifts He
has passed on to the church (v. 42):

a. The signet ring signifies the Holy Spirit
as a seal within and upon Christ's believers (Acts 2:33; Eph. 1:13; 4:30; cf. Luke
15:22).

b. The garments signify Christ as our objective righteousness for our justification before God (1 Cor. 1:30; cf. Psa. 45:9,
13; Luke 15:22) and as our subjective
righteousness lived out of us that we may
be qualified to participate in the marriage of the Lamb (Phil. 3:9; Psa. 45:14;
Rev. 19:7-9).

c. The gold chain signifies the beauty of the
Holy Spirit given for obedience expressed
in submission (cf. Acts 5:32); a chained
neck signifies a will that has been conquered and subdued to obey God's commandment (Gen. 41:42; cf. S. S. 1:10; Prov.
1:8-9).

2. According to the sequence of spiritual experience, we first receive the sealing of
the Spirit for salvation; then we receive the
garment of righteousness and begin to live
Christ (Gal. 2:20; Phil. 1:20-21a); in order for
us to live Christ, our neck must be chained,
our will must be conquered and subdued, by
the Holy Spirit.

G. After being resurrected from the prison of death
and ushered into the position of ascension, Joseph married Asenath, who portrays the church
taken out of the Gentile world during Christ's
rejection by the children of Israel (Gen. 41:45);
Joseph called the name of his firstborn Manasseh (meaning "making to forget") and his
second Ephraim (meaning "twice fruitful"); Joseph declared, "God has made me forget all my
trouble and all my father's house," and "God has

made me fruitful in the land of my affliction"
(vv. 51-52).

Day 5   II. **The record of Joseph's life is a revelation of
the rulership of the Spirit, for the rulership
of the Spirit is the reigning aspect of a mature saint; the rulership of the Spirit (a life of
reigning in life, being under the restriction
and limitation of the divine life in the reality
of God's kingdom) is higher than any other
aspect of the Spirit (Rom. 5:17, 21; 14:17-18;
cf. 2 Cor. 3:17-18; 2 Tim. 4:22; Rev. 4:1-3):**

A. Although Joseph was full of human feelings and
sentiments toward his brothers, he kept himself
with all his feelings under the rulership of the
Spirit; he dealt with his brothers soberly, wisely,
and with discernment, disciplining them according to their need in order to perfect them and
build them up that they might be a collective people living together as God's testimony on earth
(Gen. 42:9, 24; 43:30-31; 45:1-2, 24).

B. Joseph denied himself and placed himself absolutely under God's sovereign leading, conducting himself wholly for the interest of God and
His people.

C. Joseph's living under God's restriction, a portrait of the human living of Christ, manifested
the maturity and perfection of the divine life
and brought in God's kingdom (John 5:19, 30b;
7:16, 18; 14:10; Matt. 8:9-10).

D. In Joseph's dealings with his brothers, we see
that he lived a calm life, a sober life, and a dis-
cerning life with love for the brothers—a self-
denying life as the practice of the kingdom life
(Gen. 45:24; Matt. 16:24; 2 Chron. 1:10; Isa.
30:15a; Phil. 1:9; 1 Tim. 5:1-2; 1 Thes. 3:12; 4:9;
2 Thes. 1:3; Rom. 12:10; 1 John 4:9; Heb. 13:1).

E. Joseph's sentiments, feelings, considerations, and
preferences were absolutely under the rulership
and control of the Spirit (Prov. 16:32).

F. The life manifested in the story of Joseph is the resurrection life, the life of God; his sentiments were under the control of the resurrection life to meet the need of his brothers (John 11:25).

G. Joseph is a living illustration of what is revealed in the New Testament; he was a self-denying person who had no self-interest, self-enjoyment, self-feeling, self-ambition, or self-goal; everything was for God and for God's people; Joseph's self-denial, his restriction under God's sovereign hand, was the key to the practice of the kingdom life.

H. The most powerful person is the one who has the strength not to do what he is able to do—this is the real denial of the self and the genuine bearing of the cross (Matt. 16:24; cf. 26:53).

I. Joseph's realization that it was God who sent him to Egypt (even though his brothers intended evil against him—Gen. 45:5, 7; 50:19-21; cf. 41:51-52) is the reality of Paul's word in Romans 8:28-29.

J. Joseph did not need to forgive his brothers, because he did not blame them; he received as from God all that his brothers had done to him, and he comforted those who had offended him (Gen. 45:5-8; 50:15-21); what grace, and what an excellent spirit, he had!

Day 6 III. **Because Joseph suffered and denied himself, he gained the riches of the life supply (*Hymns,* #635); in order to receive food from him, the people had to pay four kinds of prices: their money, their livestock, their land, and themselves (47:14-23; cf. Rev. 3:18):**

A. Money represents convenience, livestock signifies the means of living, and land represents resources; if we would receive the life supply from the Lord as the Dispenser, we must give Him our convenience, our means of livelihood, and our resources; the more we give Him, the more life supply we will receive from Him.

   B. Ultimately, in order to receive the best portion from the Lord, including food for satisfaction and seed to produce something for others (Gen. 47:23), we must hand ourselves, every part of our being, over to Him (Lev. 1:4).

   C. When we pay the highest price by handing over every part of our being to Him, we enjoy the best portion of the enjoyment of Christ.

Morning Nourishment

Gen. You shall be over my household, and according to your
41:40-41 word all my people shall be ruled; only in the throne
will I be greater than you. Then Pharaoh said to
Joseph, See, I have set you over all the land of Egypt.

Abraham, Isaac, and Jacob with Joseph are one person.
Joseph is not a separate aspect of a complete spiritual person as
Abraham, Isaac, and Jacob are. Rather,....Joseph is an aspect of
Jacob. The Bible does not say that God is the God of Abraham,
the God of Isaac, the God of Jacob, and the God of Joseph....
There are only three. But when we come in Jacob to the stage
of maturity, we see that with the mature life there is the reigning aspect. Neither Abraham nor Isaac reigned. But Joseph
reigned representatively for Jacob. In other words, Jacob reigned
through Joseph. (*Life-study of Genesis*, p. 1408)

Today's Reading

In the last few chapters of Genesis we see an Israel expressing God's image and exercising His dominion. The exercise of
God's dominion over all things is manifested in Joseph's life,
whereas God's image is expressed in Israel....The two aspects
of expressing God's image and exercising God's dominion must
be found in one person. Therefore, what is found in Joseph's life
may be called the reigning aspect of the matured Israel.

Joseph is not a complete person but simply an aspect of a
matured saint who has passed through the experiences represented by the lives of Abraham, Isaac, and Jacob. After passing
through all these experiences, the matured saint has an aspect
that is constituted solely of Christ....Joseph represents this constituted aspect of a matured saint. In each of us there is a part
that is constituted of Christ. Even if you have just been regenerated, a part of you, your regenerated spirit, has been constituted
of Christ. This is the beginning of Christ's constitution in you.
The process of being constituted of Christ will continue until it
reaches its climax when the reigning aspect comes forth in you.

Joseph represents the reigning aspect of the mature life. As such a representative, Joseph typifies Christ, for the reigning aspect of the mature life is Christ constituted into our being.

In the presence of the Lord, Joseph was prospered by Him (Gen. 39:2-3, 23). Where the presence of the Lord is, there is not only the Lord's authority but also prosperity brought about by the Lord's sovereignty. While Joseph was undergoing ill-treatment, he enjoyed the prosperity that came to him under the Lord's sovereignty....In the Lord's presence, Joseph was favored with the Lord's blessing wherever he was....When Joseph enjoyed prosperity, he and those who were involved with him were blessed (39:4-5, 22-23).

If we do not know how to control our tears, laughter, or anger, it means that we are childish in life. The strongest sign that we are matured is that we are able to control our emotion....When the two sons of Aaron were burned in the presence of God, there were indications that Aaron was forbidden to weep (Lev. 10:1-3). Aaron might have said, "My two sons have just died in my sight, and you ask me not to weep. Moses, you are not human." Both Moses and Aaron were in the presence of the Lord. Moses could serve God in His presence because he knew how to control his feelings of sympathy for his brother. Aaron took Moses' word. Whether or not you should weep, laugh, or be angry depends upon the Lord's presence. We are not in the world but in the presence of the Lord in the Holy of Holies. When you are about to express your emotion, you should not do so according to your feeling. Rather, you must express your emotion according to God's presence....Joseph could be the ruler in Egypt because he was mature. Being mature, he ruled over himself and over the whole earth. At the right time Joseph wept regarding his brothers. Even this reveals that he was a person fully under the control of God's guidance. In Genesis 42 through 44 Joseph did not weep in the presence of his brothers. But in chapter 45, after the brothers had passed through the dealings and had learned their lessons, Joseph wept. (*Life-study of Genesis,* pp. 1409-1410, 1431, 1430, 1506-1507)

Further Reading: Life-study of Genesis, msgs. 111-112

Enlightenment and inspiration: _____

_____

_____

_____

Morning Nourishment

Gen. ...We have had a dream, and there is no one to
40:8 interpret it. And Joseph said to them, Do not interpretations belong to God? Please tell *it* to me.
41:15-16 And Pharaoh said to Joseph, I have had a dream, but
there is no one who can interpret it; and I have heard
it said of you that when you hear a dream you can interpret it. And Joseph answered Pharaoh, saying, It is
not of me; God will give Pharaoh a favorable answer.

Joseph was tested by the fact that his dreams were not fulfilled. Immediately after Joseph had his dreams, he told his parents and brothers about them. Not long after that, he was sold
into slavery and then cast into prison where, I believe, he stayed
over ten years. In his dreams there was no indication or implica-
tion that Joseph would suffer. However, immediately after Joseph
had those dreams, he had to endure suffering. Likewise, I can
testify that the throne does not immediately follow the vision
of Christ, the church, the cross, or the inner life. Instead, there
is suffering, trial, betrayal, and imprisonment.

Those of us who have been in the church life for many years
have had this experience. Perhaps some years ago you saw a
wonderful vision concerning Christ and the church life. Perhaps you even sang about the glorious church life. But what
has actually happened in the church life has not been that excellent or glorious. (*Life-study of Genesis,* pp. 1436-1437)

Today's Reading

During his imprisonment...Joseph had the faith and the boldness to interpret the dreams of his two companions in prison
even though his dreams were not yet fulfilled (Gen. 40:8-19)....It
is the same with us in the church life today. Some brothers and
sisters are what we may call old-time dreamers. They are those
who had dreams a long time ago. Although they were excited by
the visions they saw and the wonderful messages they heard,
they were later sold into Egypt. Instead of being surrounded
by sheaves, they found themselves surrounded by "Egyptian

scorpions"; and instead of being in the third heaven, they found themselves in prison. Then some latecomers joined them in prison, just as Joseph was joined in his confinement by the chief cupbearer and the baker....These latecomers also had some dreams. They could not understand their dreams, but Joseph was able to interpret them. Although Joseph's dreams had not yet been fulfilled, he had the faith and the boldness to interpret the dreams of his companions....Joseph seemed to be saying, "I had two dreams, and God gave me the interpretation of them. I still believe in these interpretations, although they have not yet been fulfilled. I have the faith to interpret your dreams for you." Do you have the boldness to say that the church life is wonderful, even when you are surrounded by some "Egyptians"? Could you say this even when your dream of the church life has not yet been fulfilled and the church life is not wonderful to you? Joseph believed not only for himself, but also for others....If your dreams have been fulfilled according to your interpretation, it is easy to interpret the dreams of others. But in Joseph's case, even after a period of about ten years, the interpretation of his own dreams had not been fulfilled. It was difficult for one in such a situation to interpret the dreams of others. Nevertheless, Joseph did so.

Andrew Murray once said a word like this: The good minister of the Word should always minister more than what he has experienced. This means that we should speak more according to the vision than according to the fulfillment of the vision. Even if our vision has not been fulfilled, we should still speak of it to others. The time will come when our vision will be fulfilled. Joseph's dreams were eventually fulfilled through his interpretation of the dream of the cupbearer.

It was just a matter of days before the dreams of the cupbearer and the baker were fulfilled. When the dreams of Joseph's companions were fulfilled, Joseph was confirmed and strengthened. (*Life-study of Genesis,* pp. 1437-1439)

Further Reading: Life-study of Genesis, msg. 112

Enlightenment and inspiration: _____

_____

_____

_____

Morning Nourishment

Gen.
41:12-13
  And a young Hebrew man was there with us, a servant of the captain of the guard. And we told him our dreams, and he interpreted *them* for us; to each one he interpreted according to his dream. And as he interpreted to us, so it happened; Pharaoh restored me to my office, and he hanged the baker.

Wherever you are, you will bring either life or death. To the cupbearer, Joseph brought life. In the cupbearer's dream we see a vine full of life. But to the baker, Joseph brought death, because the baker was devoured by birds. It is not an insignificant matter to be a Joseph, for wherever you go, people will either receive life or suffer death. Either they will go to Christ typified by the vine full of life, or they will be devoured by Satan, represented by the birds of the air. In 2 Corinthians 2:14 the apostle Paul said, "But thanks be to God, who always leads us in triumph in the Christ and manifests the savor of the knowledge of Him through us in every place." In verse 16 Paul says, "To some a savor out of death unto death, and to the others a savor out of life unto life."...No matter who a person may be, if he contacts you, it will be either life or death to him. This is a very significant matter. This is the experience of Joseph. (*Life-study of Genesis,* pp. 1442-1443)

Today's Reading

Young people, no matter how long your trial may be, do not be disappointed. You need to recognize that your trial is of God. No one can be enthroned without being tried and tested. Although we like to be enthroned immediately, God would say, "The time is not yet. Do not talk to Me about enthronement. You need to be put into the dungeon." If you seek the Lord, the Lord will put you into a dungeon. Perhaps all who are around you—your wife, your children, the elders, and the brothers and sisters—intend to respect you; however, whatever they do only serves to put you into a dungeon....Without the dungeon, we cannot ascend to the throne. Do not be a dungeon dropout; stay in the dungeon until you graduate and receive the crown.

If Joseph had not stayed in the dungeon for twelve years, he would not have been qualified to rule over the land of Egypt. For this, he had to be thirty years of age. Those twelve years in the dungeon accomplished a great deal for him, not through objective education but through subjective suffering and discipline. Be patient; eventually you will be qualified to rule.

Joseph was truly a dreamer, and his life was a life of dreams. A victorious and overcoming Christian will always be a dreamer. You need to have dreams, and you need to interpret the dreams of others. Day by day, let us all speak according to our vision, according to our dreams. Furthermore, we must interpret the visions of others, and we must live according to our vision. We should not speak according to our feelings but according to the vision. We are visionaries. Because we are visionaries, we do everything according to the vision. Although a certain thing has not yet come to pass, we speak according to what we have seen of it, and we find that our vision is being fulfilled.

What we are describing in this message is not a mere doctrine. As we follow the heavenly vision, we shall trace Joseph's footsteps. Never think that Joseph was enthroned immediately after he saw the vision. No, he had to pass through a long period of trial and testing. The visions Joseph saw not only controlled his life; they also sustained his faith. This does not mean, however, that if your faith is stronger, the length of time until the fulfillment of your dreams will be shortened. Rather, the stronger your faith is, the longer the period of testing will be. Joseph's time of testing was much longer than that of his companions because he was more valuable than they. Because they were not so valuable, the time of their fulfillment came very quickly. Actually, for those two latecomers, there was nearly no testing. They each had a dream, and a few days later their dreams were fulfilled. Because Joseph was important and valuable, the time of his testing could not be shortened. (*Life-study of Genesis,* pp. 1458-1459, 1463, 1440-1441)

Further Reading: Life-study of Genesis, msg. 114

Enlightenment and inspiration: _____

_____

_____

_____

Morning Nourishment

Gen. ...Pharaoh took off his signet ring from his hand and
41:42 put it upon Joseph's hand,...clothed him in garments
of fine linen, and put a gold chain around his neck.
51-52 And Joseph called the name of the firstborn Manasseh, for, *he said,* God has made me forget all my
trouble and all my father's house. And he called the
name of the second Ephraim, for, *he said,* God has
made me fruitful in the land of my affliction.

In his receiving glory and gifts in his enthronement, Joseph
typifies Christ, who received glory (Heb. 2:9) and gifts (Psa.
68:18; Acts 2:33) in His ascension. The ring, the garments, and
the gold chain portray the gifts that Christ received in His
ascension to the heavens, which gifts He has passed on to the
church. The signet ring signifies the Holy Spirit as a seal within
and upon Christ's believers (Acts 2:33; Eph. 1:13; 4:30; cf. Luke
15:22). The garments signify Christ as our objective righteousness for our justification before God (1 Cor. 1:30; cf. Psa. 45:9, 13;
Luke 15:22) and as our subjective righteousness lived out of us
that we may be qualified to participate in the marriage of the
Lamb (Psa. 45:14 and footnote 1; Rev. 19:7-9 and footnote 2 on
v. 8). The golden chain signifies the beauty of the Holy Spirit given
for obedience expressed in submission (cf. Acts 5:32). A chained
neck signifies a will that has been conquered and subdued to
obey God's commandment (cf. S. S. 1:10; Prov. 1:8-9). According
to the sequence of spiritual experience, we first receive the sealing Spirit for salvation; then we receive the garment of righteousness and begin to live Christ (Gal. 2:20; Phil. 1:20-21a). In
order for us to live Christ, our neck must be chained, our will
must be subdued, by the Holy Spirit. (Gen. 41:42, footnote 1)

Today's Reading

In Genesis 41:45 we see that Joseph took as his wife Asenath, the daughter of Potipherah, priest of On. Joseph's wife
was a heathen, an Egyptian. Joseph took her during the time
he was rejected by his brothers. This also is a type portraying

how Christ has taken the Gentiles as His wife during the time of His rejection by the Israelites.

In the book of Genesis we have seen three wives who portray the church: Eve, the wife of Adam; Rebekah, the wife of Isaac; and Asenath, the wife of Joseph. As the wife of Adam, Eve portrays how the church comes out of Christ and is a part of Christ. She typifies how the church is the same in life and nature as Christ and eventually becomes one Body with Him. Thus, Eve typifies the church being a part of Christ, coming out of Christ, returning to Christ, and being one with Christ. Rebekah portrays the church as the called and selected one, the one from the same source as Christ. Isaac came from a particular source, and Abraham's servant was sent to that source to select and call a wife for Isaac and to bring her to him. This selected one was Rebekah. Asenath portrays the church taken out of the Gentile world by Christ during His rejection by the children of Israel. During the time of this rejection, Christ came to the Gentile world, stayed there, and received the church out of the Gentile world.

Of his wife, Asenath, Joseph begot two sons, Manasseh and Ephraim. The name Manasseh means "making to forget"... (41:51). This indicates that with the birth of Manasseh Joseph forgot all his afflictions. When Manasseh was born, Joseph seemed to say, "Praise the Lord! He has caused me to forget my afflictions." This reveals that when the church is productive, Christ will declare that He has forgotten His afflictions.

The name of Joseph's second son was Ephraim, which means "twice fruitful" (41:52). When Ephraim was born, Joseph said, "God has made me fruitful in the land of my affliction." With Joseph, instead of affliction, there was fruitfulness. When we preach the gospel and produce fruit, Christ will be happy and declare, "There is no more affliction. But look at all the fruit!" (*Life-study of Genesis,* pp. 1453-1454)

Further Reading: Life-study of Genesis, msg. 113

Enlightenment and inspiration: _____

_____

_____

_____

Morning Nourishment

Gen.   And Joseph hurried—for his inward parts burned
43:30-31 for his brother—and sought *a place* to weep. So he
          entered into his chamber and wept there. Then
          he washed his face and came out, and he controlled
          himself and said, Serve the meal.

What we see in the life of Joseph is the rulership of the Spirit.
You may have heard of the regeneration of the Spirit, the convic-
tion of the Spirit, the inspiration of the Spirit, the infilling of the
Spirit, the anointing of the Spirit, the power of the Spirit, the
light of the Spirit, and the life of the Spirit, but the term *the rulership of the Spirit* is something new....This aspect of the Spirit
is higher than any other aspect. It is even higher than the building of the Spirit. The rulership of the Spirit is the topstone, the
capstone, of the structure of the teaching of the Spirit. The record of Joseph's life is a revelation of the rulership of the Spirit,
for the rulership of the Spirit is the reigning aspect of a matured
saint. (*Life-study of Genesis,* pp. 1469-1470)

Today's Reading

The life manifested in the story of Joseph is not the human
life, much less the fallen life. Moreover, it is not even the good
natural life. Rather, it is the resurrection life, the life of God.
Although Joseph was in an exciting situation, he did not display any looseness. This is life. With Joseph we see not only life
but also the way of life, which is to keep ourselves under control. Never think that Joseph was not human. He was full of
human feelings and sentiments, but he kept himself with all
his feelings under the rulership of the Spirit. Therefore, in
Joseph we see not only the mature life but a reigning life and
the way of this reigning life. We all, especially the young people, need such a life and such a way that is the reigning aspect
of a mature person. This life is not easily excited, and it does
not reveal its glory. Instead, in the midst of excitement it remains calm, controls itself, and conceals its glory.

Joseph's brothers were under his control, and he could have

done whatever he wanted with them. If he had wanted them beheaded, he had the authority to command it. He also could have feasted with them if he had wanted to do that. But as one representing the reigning aspect of the mature life, Joseph behaved in a proper way toward everyone. Because not all his brothers were the same, he did not treat them all in the same way. The one who was the most evil required the most thorough discipline. As a type of Christ, Joseph did the same thing to his brothers that Christ will do to the nation of Israel in the future. First, Joseph disciplined them....Joseph did everything soberly and with discernment. But this did not mean that he had no love for his brothers. On the contrary, he had a great deal of love toward them. However, at the time he could not openly display his love for them. Rather, he had to extend love to them in a secret way. He did this by restoring their money and by giving them provision for their journey (Gen. 42:25). Because Joseph's brothers did not understand his wise dealing with them, they were frightened by his secret love.

During the seven years of plenty, Joseph stored up the grain. He did not take care of his own interests. It was not an easy task to store all that grain. For seven years Joseph gathered the grain and stored it in barns. This was a big job. On the one hand, Joseph was laboring; on the other hand, he was suffering because he was separated from his father. During these seven years he did not care for himself but made arrangements for others to be taken care of in the future. What he did in the seven years of plenty was for the people. He did this at the cost of taking care of his own interests, at the cost of seeing his father.

The riches are not with the inexperienced ones. In order to be rich, we need to suffer for a long period of time. It took Joseph twenty years, from the age of seventeen to the age of thirty-seven, to become rich. Eventually, after many years of suffering, the food was in his hands. Because he had the food, all the hungry ones came to him. (*Life-study of Genesis*, pp. 1479, 1482, 1526-1527)

Further Reading: Life-study of Genesis, msgs. 115-116

Enlightenment and inspiration: _____

_____

_____

_____

Morning Nourishment

Gen. ...When that year had ended, they came to him the
47:18 second year and said to him, We cannot hide from
my lord that our money has been spent, and the
herds of cattle are my lord's. There is nothing left in
the sight of my lord except our bodies and our lands.
23 Then Joseph said to the people, Now that I have
this day bought you and your land for Pharaoh,
here is seed for you that you may sow the land.

The genuine life supply is never sold cheaply....[If you want the
supply], then you must pay the price. The concept of generosity is
a worldly concept. Joseph was in another realm, where there was
neither generosity nor scarcity, just the supply and the price....
In the Lord's recovery nothing is cheap. If you want the food, you
must pay the price. The greater the price you pay, the greater
supply you will receive. (*Life-study of Genesis*, pp. 1527-1528)

Today's Reading

The people who came to Joseph for food paid four kinds of
prices: their money, their cattle, their land, and themselves....
These four items cover all the prices we need to pay today.
When we pay with our money, cattle, lands, and ourselves, we
receive all four types of supply. The first supply is not as rare or
precious as the fourth supply. Each supply is more precious
than the previous one, and the last is the most precious of all.

According to a superficial understanding, money is what we
depend on. Actually, money represents convenience....Some are
not willing to pay the price for the supply because they are concerned about losing their conveniences....To take the way of the
Lord's recovery is costly and inconvenient. Yes, if you take this
way, you will lose your conveniences, but you will gain the supply.

The second item the people had to pay for the food supply was
their cattle....Cattle signifies the means of our living....Today
you may care very much about your automobile. Perhaps you
are afraid that it will be stolen. If so, your automobile is your
donkey. For those with a doctoral degree, their degree is their

donkey. For others their position is their donkey. But Christ, the rich One, the Supplier, is here, and He is neither generous nor stingy. Although He does not want to squeeze anything out of you, for your sake He requires that you pay a price. He will never sell His supply cheaply. After you pay your money, you need to pay with your cattle. Only by handing over your cattle will you receive the second supply.

After handing over our cattle, we need to hand over our land. The land represents our resources. The Lord Jesus is a "robber"; He "robs" His lovers of everything. He takes our money, our cattle, and our land....The Lord Jesus in His recovery "robs" us of everything—of our convenience, our means of livelihood, and our resources. If you are willing to give the Lord your lands, you will receive the third supply.

The last item the Lord requires is ourselves, including every aspect of our being. The Lord Jesus will claim every part of you. Have your ears been claimed by Him? If they have, you will not listen to anything other than Christ. Have your lips been claimed? If so, then they will be used differently. Has your whole being been claimed by the Lord Jesus? I doubt that very many have handed over their whole being to the Lord. Why are there still so many opinions, and why is there so little oneness and building in today's Christianity? It is due to the fact that very few are willing to hand themselves over to Christ.

By making the last payment, the payment of themselves, to Joseph, the people partook of the top portion....When you pay the highest price, you enjoy the best portion. Eventually, we receive not only food for satisfaction, but also seed for reproduction.

When the Lord Jesus comes, the whole earth...will belong to Christ, and we shall hand over whatever we have and whatever we are to Him....If we make the fourth payment, we shall receive not only the food to satisfy ourselves but also the seed to produce something for others. (*Life-study of Genesis,* pp. 1528-1532)

Further Reading: Life-study of Genesis, msgs. 118-120

Enlightenment and inspiration: _____

_____

_____

_____

Hymns, #942

1 God's Kingdom on the earth is now
His sovereign government within;
'Tis Christ Himself in us to live
As Lord and King to rule and reign.

2 His life with His authority
Enthrones Him now within our hearts
To govern all our words and deeds
And regulate our inward parts.

3 The Lord enthroned within our hearts
His Kingdom doth establish there,
Assuring His full right to reign
And for God's purpose to prepare.

4 'Tis by His reign within our hearts
That life to us He e'er supplies;
When taking Him as Lord and King,
His wealth our being satisfies.

5 'Tis by His ruling from within
His fulness vast is testified;
'Tis when His inner kingdom rules
His Body's blessed and edified.

6 'Tis by His heav'nly rule within
As heav'nly citizens we live;
'Tis by submission to His rule
Expression of His reign we give.

7 Here in this heav'nly realm we live,
And with this heav'nly pow'r possessed
We walk and fight in heav'nly light
Until the Kingdom's manifest.

Composition for prophecy with main point and sub-points: _____

Blessing

Scripture Reading: Gen. 47:7, 10; 48:9, 14-16, 20; Heb. 5:6; 7:7; 11:21; Num. 6:22-27; 2 Cor. 13:14

Day 1 **I. To be transformed is to be metabolically changed in our natural life, to be mature is to be filled with the divine life that changes us, and blessing is the overflow of life:**

A. As Jacob was about to bless the two sons of Joseph, he spoke of the Triune God in his experience (Gen. 48:9, 15-16):

  1. The God before whom Abraham and Isaac walked is the Father.

  2. The God who shepherded Jacob "all my life to this day" is the Spirit.

  3. The Angel who redeemed him from all evil is the Son.

B. Jacob realized that his destiny and existence were absolutely in the hands of the shepherding God; the experience of the Triune God is so that we may bless others with the Triune God.

Day 2 **II. The strongest sign of Jacob's maturity was his blessing of others:**

A. The first thing Jacob did after arriving in Egypt was to bless Pharaoh (47:7, 10); according to Hebrews 7:7, "the lesser is blessed by the greater"; this is a proof that in God's sight Jacob was greater than Pharaoh.

B. In order to bless others, we must be filled to the brim with life so that life overflows to them; Jacob's mature life was filled with blessings; he blessed Pharaoh, the two sons of Joseph (Gen. 48:8-20), and his own sons (49:1-28); those blessings of his sons were prophecies related to the destiny of the twelve tribes of Israel.

III. The principle of blessing is that the greater blesses the lesser (Heb. 7:7):

A. To be greater or lesser is not a matter of age but a matter of the measure of Christ; we are greater or lesser according to our measure of Christ.

B. Although John the Baptist was so close to Christ, he did not have Christ within him; those in the kingdom of the heavens are not only close to Christ but also have Christ within them; for this reason, the least in the kingdom of the heavens is greater than John (Matt. 11:11).

C. If by having more of Christ we are greater than others, then we are qualified to bless them, for the greater always blesses the lesser.

D. To bless others means to minister Christ to them; we bless people with the very Christ in whom we participate and whom we enjoy; if we enjoy Christ more, we have more of Christ to minister to others.

Day 3   IV. **The meaning of blessing is that blessing is the overflow of God through someone's maturity in life:**

A. God cannot flow Himself into others without a human channel; the only humanity that God can use as a channel is the one saturated and permeated with God (Phil. 1:23-25).

B. Maturity in life is a matter of being filled with God; when we are full of God, we have the overflow of God, and thus we are able to bless everyone we meet.

V. **The first case of blessing in the Bible is Melchizedek's blessing of Abraham (Gen. 14:18-20); Melchizedek is a type of Christ (Heb. 5:6):**

A. Blessing is the overflow of God, and this overflow is brought to people through the priests; we all need to be priests (Rev. 1:6; 1 Pet. 2:5, 9), those who bring people to God.

B. If we would bless others, we must be close to God ourselves; people need God's blessing, because they are far away from Him.

C. A priest eliminates the distance between God

and the people; he brings those who are far off
into the presence of God (cf. Exo. 28:9-12, 15-21).

D. Before we are blessed by a priest, there may
be a distance between us and God, but after he
blesses us, this distance is taken away, and we
are brought into the presence of God to share
in the enjoyment of God.

Day 4 VI. **In Numbers 6:22-27 we see a pattern of blessing by the priests; this blessing is neither
an Old Testament blessing nor a New Testament blessing; rather, it is the eternal blessing of the Triune God, which is the Triune
God dispensing Himself in His Divine Trinity into us for our enjoyment:**

A. *Jehovah bless you and keep you* can be ascribed
to the Father (v. 24):

1. The Father blesses us in every way and in
every aspect in His love (cf. Eph. 1:3), and He
keeps us in every way and in every aspect in
His power (cf. John 17:11, 15; 1 Pet. 1:5).

2. The Lord prayed that the Father would
keep us in His name (John 17:11); this is
to keep us in the dispensing Triune God; the
Lord Jesus went on to pray that the Father
would keep us out of the hands of the evil
one (v. 15).

3. We should pray for the blessing of being kept
absolutely in the dispensing of the Triune
God and altogether outside of the evil one;
what a blessing this is!

B. *Jehovah make His face shine upon you and be
gracious to you* can be ascribed to the Son (Num.
6:25):

1. In Luke 1:78, when the Lord Jesus was about
to be born, Zachariah prophesied, "The rising
sun will visit us from on high"; the rising sun
is the Son in the Divine Trinity; this implies
God's incarnation to show Himself to us in a
shining way (Matt. 4:16; John 8:12).

2. The word *face* in Numbers 6:25 signifies presence; as the One whose face shines upon us, Christ the Son is the visible presence of the invisible God (2 Pet. 1:16-18; Matt. 17:1-2).

3. Numbers 6:25 speaks not only of Jehovah making His face shine upon us but also of Jehovah being gracious to us; these two points added together equal John 1:14, 16-17.

4. God's incarnation was the shining of His presence, and along with this shining, there was grace; this grace is the grace of the Lord Jesus Christ, which is actually Christ Himself (2 Cor. 13:14).

C. *Jehovah lift up His countenance upon you and give you peace* can be ascribed to the Spirit (Num. 6:26):

1. The face denotes the presence of the person, and the countenance denotes the expression of the person; to lift up our countenance upon a person means that we confirm, assure, promise, and give everything to that person.

2. Jesus came as the face of God, and the Holy Spirit comes as the countenance of God; if we grieve Him, His countenance will drop (Eph. 4:30), but if we obey Him, He will be happy with us, and He will lift up His countenance to confirm us, assure us, guarantee us, promise us, and give us everything.

Day 5 VII. **The blessing of the apostle Paul is seen in 2 Corinthians 13:14—"the grace of the Lord Jesus Christ and the love of God and the fellowship of the Holy Spirit be with you all":**

A. In the blessing of the apostle Paul, the Triune God comes to people for their enjoyment; Paul not only brought people into the presence of God but also brought God into them.

B. On the one hand, to bless others is to bring them into the presence of God; on the other hand, it is to bring God into them as love, grace, and fellowship so that they may enjoy the Triune God— the Father, the Son, and the Spirit.

C. Love, grace, and fellowship are three stages of God for our enjoyment—love is within, grace is love expressed, and fellowship is the transmission of grace into us.

D. The love of God is the source, since God is the origin; the grace of the Lord is the course of the love of God, since the Lord is the expression of God; and the fellowship of the Spirit is the impartation of the grace of the Lord with the love of God, since the Spirit is the transmission of the Lord with God, for our experience and enjoyment of the Triune God—the Father, the Son, and the Holy Spirit, with Their divine virtues.

E. The divine revelation of the Divine Trinity in the holy Word is not for theological study but for the apprehending of how God in His mysterious and marvelous Divine Trinity dispenses Himself into His chosen people, that we as His chosen and redeemed people may, as indicated by the apostle's blessing to the Corinthian believers, participate in, experience, enjoy, and possess the processed Triune God now and for eternity.

VIII. **The Lord's blessing crosses man's natural maneuvering (Gen. 48:13-20):**

A. Most of the time our choosing leads to maneuvering, and God's crossing hand comes in to bless the one we did not choose; the shifting of the birthright from Manasseh to Ephraim shows that the Lord's blessing does not depend on man's natural maneuvering but on God's desire and selection.

B. In any selection that we make, there is the possibility of maneuvering according to our taste and choice; we must not maneuver, and we must not be disappointed; rather, we must believe that the Lord's hand will cross over to us.

C. Man's natural concept holds back the Lord's blessing hand (vv. 17-20); the one we think is the best may turn out to be the worst, but one of the opposers may become today's apostle Paul; many will be raised up who do not fit our concept.

Day 6 IX. **Jacob's supplanting hands eventually became blessing hands (25:26; 47:7, 10; 48:14-16; Heb. 11:21):**

A. In Genesis 25 we see that Jacob began his supplanting even when he was in his mother's womb, but in Genesis 47 and 48 we see that these two supplanting hands have become blessing hands, bringing people into God's presence and ministering God into them so that they may enjoy Him.

B. A supplanter, a heel holder, became the greatest person on the earth at that time; he had become able to bless Pharaoh because he had become greater than Pharaoh; he became this kind of person by the way of life.

C. We need the growth in life and the maturity in life so that we may be filled with Christ to become those who are able to bless others.

X. **At the time of Genesis 49, when Jacob prophesied concerning his twelve sons with blessing, he was a God-man, a man filled, constituted, permeated, and even reorganized with God; whatever he thought was God's thought, and whatever opinion he expressed was God's opinion (cf. 1 Cor. 7:10, 12, 25, 40):**

A. In order to prophesy with blessing, we must know God, the desire of God's heart, and the purpose of God.

B. In order to prophesy with blessing, we must know people; that is, we must know the actual situation of every person involved.
C. In order to prophesy with blessing, we must be full of the riches of Christ.
D. In order to prophesy with blessing, we must have a strong, active spirit.

Morning Nourishment

Gen. And he [Jacob] blessed Joseph and said, The God
48:15-16 before whom my fathers Abraham and Isaac
walked, the God who has shepherded me all my life
to this day, the Angel who has redeemed me from
all evil, bless the boys; and may my name be named
on them, and the name of my fathers Abraham and
Isaac; and may they be a teeming multitude in the
midst of the earth.

[In Genesis 37:1] Jacob was a transformed person, but he
was not yet mature. To be transformed is to be metabolically
changed in our natural life (Rom. 12:2; 2 Cor. 3:18); to be mature is to be filled with the divine life that changes us. We may
be changed in our natural life (transformed) yet not be filled
with the divine life (mature). The last stage of transformation
is maturity. Jacob's transformation began at the time God
touched him (Gen. 32:25), and it continued until the end of
chapter 36, when the process of transformation was relatively
complete (see footnote 1 on Gen. 37:3). Genesis 37:1—43:14 is
a record of the process of Jacob's maturity.

Genesis shows a complete picture of how human beings
can be remade and transformed to express God in His image
and represent God with His dominion. This book ends as it
begins—with God's image and dominion. The last fourteen
chapters indicate that after Jacob had become Israel, he bore
the image of God and, through Joseph, exercised the dominion
of God. For God's expression and dominion there is the need of
maturity. Only a mature life can bear God's image and exercise His dominion. (Gen. 37:1, footnote 1)

Today's Reading

The strongest manifestation of Jacob's maturity in life is
the fact that Jacob blessed everyone, including Pharaoh (Gen.
47:7, 10), Jacob's two grandsons (ch. 48), and his own twelve sons
(49:1-28). Jacob's supplanting hands became blessing hands
(48:14-16). Maturity in life is a matter of being filled with God

as life, and blessing is the overflow of life, the overflow of God through the maturity in life. To bless others is to bring them into the presence of God and to bring God into them as grace, love, and fellowship that they may enjoy the Triune God—the Father, the Son, and the Spirit (14:18-19; Num. 6:23-27; 2 Cor. 13:14). That Jacob blessed Pharaoh indicates that he was greater than Pharaoh (Heb. 7:7). (Gen. 47:7, footnote 1)

When Jacob went to Egypt, he did not engage in any activity for himself. This also is a manifestation of his maturity. Do not think that Jacob was lazy, tired, or lacked the energy to act. If he had not been able to do anything, he could have ordered his sons to do things for him. However, he did not do this. Rather, he was fully satisfied and rested absolutely in God's sovereignty. He did not depend upon his own endeavors. From his experience through the years, he had come to know that his destiny was in the hands of God, not in his own hands. As Jacob was about to bless the two sons of Joseph, he spoke of God as the One who had shepherded him all his life long (Gen. 48:15-16). Jacob's word in 48:15 and 16 is a reference to the Triune God. Here we see the Triune God in Jacob's experience, not in doctrine....Here we see a threefold mention of God....The God before whom Abraham and Isaac walked must be the Father; the God who shepherded Jacob his whole life must be the Spirit; and the Angel who redeemed him from all evil must be the Son. This is the Triune God in Jacob's experience.

Jacob experienced God's sovereign, shepherding care. Shepherding includes feeding. The shepherd meets every need of the sheep, who only eat and rest. Every provision for their existence comes from the shepherd. The example of the shepherd is a marvelous illustration of Jacob's realization that his destiny and existence were absolutely in the hands of the shepherding God. Thus, after he had matured and had arrived in Egypt, he did nothing for himself. This is another sign of the maturity of life. (*Life-study of Genesis,* pp. 1210-1211)

Further Reading: Life-study of Genesis, msg. 94

Enlightenment and inspiration: _____

_____

_____

_____

Morning Nourishment

Gen. And Joseph brought in Jacob his father and set him
47:7 before Pharaoh, and Jacob blessed Pharaoh.
Heb. But without any dispute the lesser is blessed by the
7:7 greater.
Gen. And Joseph said to his father, They are my sons,
48:9 whom God has given to me here. And he said, Bring
them to me, please, that I may bless them.

The strongest sign of Jacob's maturity [was] his blessing
of others. The first thing Jacob did after arriving in Egypt
was bless Pharaoh (Gen. 47:7, 10). Although Pharaoh was the
highest person on earth, he was under Jacob's blessing hand.
According to Hebrews 7:7, "the lesser is blessed by the greater."
Thus, the fact that Jacob blessed Pharaoh was a proof that he
was greater than Pharaoh. After Jacob had been ushered into
Pharaoh's presence, he did not speak to him in a polite, political
way. He stretched forth his hand and blessed him. This is absolutely different from human culture and religion. As Jacob was
leaving Pharaoh's presence, he blessed him again. (*Life-study
of Genesis*, p. 1211)

Today's Reading

Blessing is the overflow of life, the overflow of God through
someone's maturity in life. In order to bless others, we must be
filled to the brim with life so that life overflows to them. Having such an overflow of life, Jacob blessed Pharaoh and the
two sons of Joseph (Gen. 48:8-20).

Jacob's mature life was filled with blessings. Jacob blessed
his twelve sons, and those blessings were prophecies relating to
the destiny of the twelve tribes of Israel. Jacob was so filled
with life that he overflowed blessings to everyone he met. This
is the strongest manifestation of Jacob's maturity in life.

[In Hebrews 7:7] we see the principle of blessing: that the
greater blesses the lesser. To be greater or lesser is not mainly a
matter of age. It is a matter of the measure of Christ. We are
greater or lesser according to our measure of Christ. In Matthew

11:11 the Lord Jesus said, "Truly I say to you, Among those born of women there has not arisen one greater than John the Baptist, yet he who is least in the kingdom of the heavens is greater than he." Here the Lord Jesus says that John the Baptist was greater than all who had preceded him. However, the least in the kingdom of heaven is greater than John. The reason John was greater than his predecessors was that he was very close to Christ. Although Abraham was great, he did not see Christ. However, John the Baptist saw Him. But, although John was so close to Christ, he did not have Christ in him. Those in the kingdom of heaven are not only close to Christ; they have Christ within them. For this reason the least in the kingdom of heaven is greater than John. The great ones in the Old Testament could say that Christ was coming, and John the Baptist could say that Christ was in front of him. But all of us in the kingdom of heaven can say that Christ is within us. We can even say, "For to me, to live is Christ" (Phil. 1:21). Hence, we are closer to Christ than John the Baptist and all who went before him.

Whether we are greater or lesser depends upon our measure of Christ. If you have more of Christ, you are greater. If you have less of Christ, you are lesser. If by having more of Christ we are greater than others, then we are qualified to bless them; for the greater always blesses the lesser. The reason for this is that the greater one has a larger measure of Christ to give to others. If you are greater than I, it means that you have a greater portion of Christ than I. If so, then you have something more of Christ to minister to me. To bless others means to minister Christ to them. Those who have just a small measure of Christ need the blessing of those who have a greater measure. We bless them with the very Christ in whom we participate and whom we enjoy. If we enjoy Christ more, then we have more of Christ to minister to others. This ministering of Christ is blessing. (*Life-study of Genesis*, pp. 1211-1214)

Further Reading: Life-study of Genesis, msg. 95

Enlightenment and inspiration: _____

_____

_____

_____

Morning Nourishment

Phil. **And being confident of this, I know that I will re-**
1:25 **main and continue with you all for your progress**
and joy of the faith.
Gen. **And Melchizedek the king of Salem brought out**
14:18-20 **bread and wine. Now he was priest of God the Most**
High. And he blessed him and said, Blessed be
Abram of God the Most High, Possessor of heaven
and earth; and blessed be God the Most High...

Blessing is the overflow of God through someone's maturity
in life. God cannot flow Himself into others without a human
channel. If Christ had never been incarnated, God would not
have been able to flow to man, because there would not have
been a channel. God's flowing needs humanity as a channel. The
only humanity God can use as the channel is one saturated and
permeated with God. For this reason Jacob did not bless anyone
until he had become mature. Jacob did not bless Laban or Esau.
Even when he saw his brother Esau after the twenty years with
Laban, he did not bless him. It was not until he went down into
Egypt that he blessed Pharaoh, the highest ruler on earth (Gen.
47:7, 10). At that time Jacob was filled with God. Through Jacob's
blessing of Pharaoh God's blessing overflowed to Pharaoh.

A child two years of age cannot bless anyone; however, a
child of seven or eight may perform some kind of blessing. This
illustrates the fact that blessing others depends upon maturity
in life. Maturity in life is a matter of being filled with God.
When you are full of God, you have the overflow of God, and
thus you are able to bless everyone you meet. (*Life-study of
Genesis*, pp. 1214-1215)

Today's Reading

The first case of blessing in the Bible is Melchizedek's blessing
of Abraham (Gen. 14:18-20). Melchizedek was a type of Christ.
Therefore, Melchizedek's coming to Abraham was Christ's coming to him. Melchizedek came to Abraham with bread and
wine, just as the Lord also comes to us with bread and wine.

Furthermore, Melchizedek came as the eternal priest, and Christ became a priest according to the eternal order of Melchizedek (Heb. 5:6). A priest brings people to God. If you would bless others, you must be God's priest. Later we shall see that in the Old Testament God commanded the priests to bless His people. Blessing is the overflow of God, and this overflow is brought to people through the priests. The first blessing was bestowed by a priest. We all need to be priests, those who bring people to God.

If we would bless others, we must be close to God ourselves. We must be priests who bring others to God. People need God's blessing because they are far away from Him. A priest eliminates the distance between God and the people; he brings those who are far off into the presence of God. On the shoulders of the high priest were two onyx stones engraved with the names of the twelve tribes of Israel, and on his breastplate there were twelve stones, also engraved with the names of the twelve tribes (Exo. 28:9-12, 15-21). Whenever the high priest entered into the Holy of Holies, he wore the breastplate and the shoulder plates. This indicated that he brought the people of Israel into the presence of God. We all realize that a priest serves God, but we may never have seen that he also eliminates the distance between the people and God. Before you are blessed by a priest, there may be a distance between you and God. But after he blesses you, this distance is taken away, and you are brought into the presence of God to share in the enjoyment of God. When Melchizedek blessed Abraham, that blessing brought him into the presence of God. Melchizedek even said, "Blessed be Abram of God the Most High" (Gen. 14:19). If you read Genesis 14 carefully, you will see that Melchizedek blessed Abraham with nothing other than God. He did not say, "Be blessed with a good house"; neither did he say, "Be blessed with two sons." Instead, he said, "Be blessed of God the Most High." In this way, Melchizedek brought Abraham much closer to God. (*Life-study of Genesis,* pp. 1215-1216)

Further Reading: Life-study of Genesis, msg. 96

Enlightenment and inspiration: _____

_____

_____

_____

Morning Nourishment

Num.   ...Thus you shall bless the children of Israel; you
6:23-26 shall say to them, Jehovah bless you and keep you;
         Jehovah make His face shine upon you and be gra-
         cious to you; Jehovah lift up His countenance upon
         you and give you peace.

In Numbers 6:23-27 we see a pattern of blessing. Here God commanded the priests to bless the people....The blessing is threefold because it is a matter of the dispensing of God into man. This involves the Trinity: the Father, the Son, and the Spirit. (*Life-study of Genesis*, p. 1216)

The blessing in Numbers 6 is neither an Old Testament blessing nor a New Testament blessing. Rather, it is the eternal blessing of the Triune God, which is the Triune God dispensing Himself in His Divine Trinity into us for our enjoyment. This is God's eternal blessing. (*Life-study of Numbers*, p. 80)

Today's Reading

Referring to the Father, Numbers 6:24 says, "Jehovah bless you and keep you." The Father blesses us in every way and in every aspect in His love (cf. Eph. 1:3), and He keeps us in every way and in every aspect in His power (cf. John 17:11, 15).

In Numbers 6:24 the word *keep* is of crucial importance. In John 17:11 the Lord Jesus prayed that the Father would keep us in His name. This is to keep us in the dispensing Triune God. While the Triune God is dispensing Himself into us, we are kept in the dispensing One. In John 17:15 the Lord Jesus went on to pray that the Father would keep us from the evil one. When we are kept in the dispensing Triune God, there is nothing left for the hand of the enemy. We should pray for the blessing of being kept absolutely in the dispensing Triune God and altogether outside of the evil one.

The second part of this blessing says, "Jehovah make His face shine upon you and be gracious to you" (Num. 6:25). In Luke 1:78...Zachariah prophesied, "The rising sun will visit us from on high." This rising sun is the Son in the Divine Trinity. This implies God's incarnation to show Himself to us in a shining way.

No one has ever seen God, but through His incarnation we have seen His face and have beheld His glory (John 1:14), and He has been shining upon us continually. Wherever He went, He was a great light shining upon the people sitting in darkness (Matt. 4:16), for He is the light of the world (John 8:12).

The word *face* in Numbers 6:25 signifies presence. As the One whose face shines upon us, Christ the Son is the visible presence of the invisible God. God and His presence are invisible, but through His incarnation He became the shining sun. This shining sun is God's invisible presence becoming visible....On the Mount of Transfiguration, some of the Lord's disciples beheld Him in His glory (2 Pet. 1:16-18; Matt. 17:1-2).

Numbers 6:25 speaks not only of Jehovah making His face to shine upon us, but also of Jehovah being gracious to us. These two points added together equal John 1:14, 16-17. God's incarnation was the shining of His presence. Along with this shining there was grace. "The Word became flesh and tabernacled among us...full of grace" (v. 14). The Lord is gracious to us; He has even become grace to us. For the Lord to be gracious to us means that He is continually grace to us. This grace is the grace of Christ (2 Cor. 13:14a), which is actually Christ Himself. When we have Christ, we have grace. The Triune God is altogether gracious to us. Day after day we enjoy Him as grace.

The third part of this blessing says, "Jehovah lift up His countenance upon you and give you peace" (Num. 6:26)....There is a difference between [the face (v. 25) and the countenance (v. 26)]. The face denotes the presence of the person, and the countenance denotes the expression of the person....Jesus came as the face of God, and the Holy Spirit comes as the countenance of God....If we grieve [the Holy Spirit (Eph. 4:30)], His countenance will drop. If we obey Him, He will be happy with us, and He will lift up His countenance to confirm us, assure us, guarantee us, promise us, and give us everything. (*Life-study of Numbers,* pp. 80-82)

Further Reading: Life-study of Numbers, msg. 11

Enlightenment and inspiration: _____

_____

_____

_____

Morning Nourishment

2 Cor. The grace of the Lord Jesus Christ and the love of God
13:14 and the fellowship of the Holy Spirit be with you all.
Gen. And he blessed them that day, saying, By you Israel
48:20 will pronounce blessings, saying, God make you like
Ephraim and like Manasseh. Thus he set Ephraim
before Manasseh.

A priest brings people to God. An apostle, however, brings God to people; he comes to people with God. In 2 Corinthians 13:14 we see a gracious visitation of the Triune God. In the blessing of the apostle Paul, the Triune God comes to people for their enjoyment. This enjoyment is the love of God as the grace of Christ by the fellowship of the Holy Spirit. Love, grace, and fellowship are not three separate things; they are three aspects or stages of one thing. They are the three stages of God for our enjoyment. Love is within, grace is love expressed, and fellowship is the transmission of grace into us. Love is within God Himself. When this love is expressed, it is grace, and grace is transmitted in the fellowship. I may love a certain brother, but this love is within me....I may express it by giving him a Bible. The Bible represents grace as the expression of the love I have within me for this brother. In order to communicate this grace to him, I must actually hand the Bible to him. This is fellowship. (*Life-study of Genesis,* pp. 1217-1218)

Today's Reading

When Joseph brought his sons Manasseh and Ephraim to Jacob, he maneuvered the situation so that the firstborn, Manasseh, would be in front of Jacob's right hand. The father put the firstborn in front of the grandfather's right hand to receive the first blessing and the second in front of the left hand to receive the second blessing. Joseph's maneuvering was according to the natural concept. According to the natural concept, Joseph was right. However, Jacob crossed his hands. Although his eyes were dim, he was very clear in his spirit. Genesis 48:17 says, "And when Joseph saw that his father laid his right hand upon the head of Ephraim, it displeased him; and he took hold of his father's hand to remove it from

Ephraim's head onto Manasseh's head." Then Joseph said, "Not so, my father, for this is the firstborn. Put your right hand upon his head" (v. 18). Jacob refused and said, "I know, my son, I know" (v. 19). Thus, the Lord's blessing crossed man's maneuvering.

In the church life I have come to have no trust in my choice. Often my hand has been held back in the choice of elders, deacons, and the leading ones in the church service because I have no trust in my discernment. Most of the time our choosing leads to maneuvering, and God's crossing hand comes in to bless the one we did not choose. Those who are parents and those who are leading ones in the church service must be careful about their choosing. Do not exercise any kind of maneuvering according to your likes and dislikes, for God's blessing always crosses our maneuvering.

Although we never know where the spiritual blessing will go, we do know that the blessing hand of the Lord always crosses man's natural maneuvering....The Lord's crossing His hands may be evil in your eyes, but it is altogether beautiful in His eyes. Blessing does not depend on your maneuvering; it depends on God's desire and selection. In any selection we make there is the possibility of maneuvering according to our taste or choice. Do not maneuver, and do not be disappointed. Rather, believe that the Lord's hand will cross over to you.

We have seen that Joseph tried to hold back his father's blessing hand. This indicates that man's natural concept holds back the Lord's blessing hand. In the church life, the Lord will raise up many we do not like, and some of them will become the best elders. Surely I have had my human feelings, concepts, and tastes. But my natural concepts have been crossed out. We simply do not know from which direction Saul of Tarsus will come. The one you think is the best may turn out to be the worst. But one of the opposers will become today's apostle Paul. Although you do not like him, the Lord likes him. Many will be raised up who do not fit your concept. (*Life-study of Genesis*, pp. 1219-1221)

Further Reading: Life-study of Philippians, msg. 7

Enlightenment and inspiration: _____

_____

_____

_____

Morning Nourishment

Gen. But Israel stretched *out* his right hand and laid *it*
48:14 *upon* Ephraim's head—although he was the youn-
ger—and his left hand upon Manasseh's head, guid-
ing his hands with insight, even though Manasseh
was the firstborn.
1 Cor. But she is more blessed if she so remains, accord-
7:40 ing to my opinion; but I think that I also have the
Spirit of God.

Jacob's supplanting hands eventually became blessing hands
(Gen. 25:26; 47:7, 10; 48:14-16). In Genesis 25 we see that Jacob
began his supplanting even when he was in his mother's womb.
How skillful he was in supplanting! But in chapters 47 and 48
we see that these two supplanting hands have become blessing
hands, bringing people into God's presence and ministering
God into people so that they may enjoy Him....Here we see the
growth and maturity in life. A supplanter, a heel-holder, became the greatest person on earth at the time. He was able to
bless Pharaoh because he had become greater than Pharaoh.
He became this kind of person by the way of life. We need the
growth in life and the maturity in life so that we may be filled
with Christ to become those who are able to bless others. (*Life-
study of Genesis*, p. 1222)

Today's Reading

Although we are familiar with what it means to prophesy, we
may not be familiar with prophesying with blessing. Genesis 49
is the only chapter that reveals this matter. Although Moses'
blessing in Deuteronomy 33 is close to what is found in Genesis
49, the blessing there is not as rich as the blessing here....The
prophesying in chapter 49 is a manifestation of maturity, for our
speaking always reveals where we are and how mature we are.

In order to prophesy with blessing, we must fulfill four requirements. The first requirement is to know God, the desire of
God's heart, and the purpose of God. God, God's desire, and God's
purpose are all revealed through Jacob's word in this chapter.

The second requirement is to know people, to know the actual situation of every person involved. You may think that, because it should be easy for a father to know his son, it was easy for Jacob to know his twelve sons. However, it is often very difficult for parents to truly know their children....Seemingly, we parents know our children; actually, we know neither what they are nor where they are. But Jacob had a thorough understanding of his sons. Every situation, condition, and hidden problem was clear in his sight. Likewise, if we would speak such a word in the church, we must know the church, the elders, and all the brothers and sisters. This is not easy....We should not know people according to our mental understanding; rather, we must know them according to the spirit.

Although we may know God, God's heart, and God's purpose and although we may know the situation of others, we shall still not be able to bless them if we are poor....[Jacob] was full of riches. Because he had no lack of riches, he could bless others.

In addition to the three requirements already covered, we need a strong, active spirit. Jacob's word in this chapter was spoken as he was dying....In his body he was dying, but in his spirit he was [vigorous,] strong and active. Therefore, in order to prophesy with blessing, we must have the knowledge of God, the knowledge of people and their situations, the riches of God, and a strong spirit.

[In 1 Corinthians 7] Paul's opinion was God's word. In principle, it is the same with Jacob in Genesis 49. Whatever Jacob uttered...was God's word. Although it was his opinion, it was also the word of God....[Verses 3 and 4 were] the utterance of a man who was filled with God, a man who had been constituted with God in his entire being....Jacob was a God-man, a man filled, constituted, permeated, and even reorganized with God. Thus, whatever he spoke was God's word; whatever he thought was God's thought; and whatever opinion he expressed was God's opinion. (*Life-study of Genesis,* pp. 1231, 1235-1236, 1239)

Further Reading: Life-study of Genesis, msg. 97

Enlightenment and inspiration: _____

_____

_____

_____

Hymns, #846

1 Oh, may my spirit flow,
    Oh, may it flow!
Now I beseech Thee, Lord,
    Oh, may it flow!
My past I would forsake,
The iron walls would break,
My spirit free would make;
    Oh, may it flow!

2 Oh, may my spirit flow,
    Oh, may it flow!
Now I implore Thee, Lord,
    Oh, may it flow!
No more self-satisfied,
No more in self-bound pride,
No more my spirit tied;
    Oh, may it flow!

3 Oh, may my spirit flow,
    Oh, may it flow!
For this I plead with Thee,
    Oh, may it flow!
High-minded not to be,
Pride shall not prison me,
I'd flow unceasingly,
    In spirit flow.

4 Oh, may my spirit flow,
    Oh, may it flow!
For this I seek Thee, Lord,
    Oh, may it flow!
No more to isolate,
Nor self to perfect make,
My spirit nought abate,
    Deeply to flow.

5 Oh, may my spirit flow,
    Oh, may it flow!
I ask Thee, gracious Lord,
    Oh, may it flow!
My trust in self o'erthrow,
Down from self's throne I'll go,
That living water flow
    In spirit, Lord.

6   Oh, may my spirit flow,
        Oh, may it flow!
    Answer my prayer, dear Lord,
        Oh, may it flow!
    Not just commune with Thee,
    I long to builded be,
    Mingle with others free
        In spirit, Lord.

Composition for prophecy with main point and sub-points: _____

_____

_____

_____

_____

_____

_____

_____

_____

_____

_____

_____

_____

_____

_____

_____

_____

_____

_____

_____

_____

_____

_____

_____

_____

_____

_____

_____

_____

Jacob's Prophesying with Blessing
(1)

Scripture Reading: Gen. 49:1-15

Day 1   I. **Jacob's twelve sons eventually became the twelve tribes of Israel, a type of the church as God's house, the Israel of God, composed of all the believers (Gal. 6:16; 1 Tim. 3:15; Heb. 3:5-6):**

A. Jacob's maturity in life, the zenith of his life, issued in the overflow of life, his prophesying with blessing for the building up of God's house (Prov. 4:18; Gen. 47:7, 10; 48:14-16; 49:1-28; 47:31; Heb. 11:21; cf. 1 Cor. 14:4b, 31).

B. Whatever was spoken prophetically by Jacob concerning his sons is a type, a picture, of the church and should be applied to the church and to the spiritual experience of the believers, as well as to the sons of Israel (cf. 10:6).

II. **The prophecy concerning Reuben is a warning concerning the defilement of fleshly lust, and the prophecy concerning Simeon and Levi is a warning concerning the destruction of the natural disposition (Gen. 49:3-7):**

A. Although Reuben had the preeminence of the birthright, because of his defilement he lost the birthright and became in danger of dying or of being greatly decreased; this should be a solemn warning to us (vv. 3-4; cf. Eph. 5:5; Matt. 1:2; Deut. 33:6; 1 Cor. 6:17-20; 1 Thes. 4:3-8; 1 Cor. 9:27; Phil. 1:20; Rom. 6:12-14; 8:2; 12:2; 16:20; 2 Tim. 2:22).

Day 2   B. Because of their cruelty according to their disposition, Simeon and Levi received no blessing from Jacob (Gen. 49:5-6; 34:25-30; cf. Deut. 22:6-7); rather, Jacob exercised his judgment over them to scatter them among the children of Israel (Gen. 49:7) so that they would not be able to behave cruelly according to their disposition (Josh. 19:1, 9; 21:1-3, 41):

1. Later, Levi used his disposition in a renewed, transformed way to slay the worshippers of the golden calf; our natural disposition can be useful if three conditions are met: consecration, using our natural disposition against our natural desire, and using it in a renewed and transformed way (Exo. 32:26-28).

2. Because of his absoluteness, desperation, and faithfulness toward God, Levi received the blessing of the priesthood with the Urim and the Thummim (Deut. 33:8-9; Exo. 32:26-28).

Day 3 III. **The prophecy concerning Judah portrays Christ in the four Gospels (the contents of the gospel), the prophecy concerning Zebulun portrays the shipping out of the gospel in the Acts (borne by the wind of the Holy Spirit), and the prophecy concerning Issachar portrays the practice of the church life in the Epistles and Revelation (for God's building) (Gen. 49:8-15):**

A. The prophecy concerning Judah portrays the good news of Christ—the victory of Christ (vv. 8-9), the kingdom of Christ (v. 10), and the enjoyment and rest in Christ (vv. 11-12); these three truths are a summary of the New Testament:

1. Judah, likened poetically to a young lion, is a type of Christ as the ultimate Overcomer (v. 9; Rev. 5:5):

a. In His victory Christ is typified as a young lion overcoming the enemies and couching in satisfaction after enjoying the prey (Gen. 49:9a); this is a picture of the victory of Christ over His enemies in His crucifixion (Col. 2:15; Heb. 2:14) and of His satisfaction and rest in His ascension as the issue of His victory (Eph. 4:8).

Day 4

   b. Christ is also the producing lioness, bring-
      ing forth many overcomers as His "lion
      cubs" (Gen. 49:9b; cf. Prov. 28:1; Rev. 22:5).
   c. That no one dares to rouse Judah up (Gen.
      49:9b) signifies that Christ's terrifying
      power in His resurrection and ascension
      has subdued everything (Matt. 28:18; Phil.
      2:9; Eph. 1:21-23).
2. In His authority and kingship Christ comes
   as the Peace Bringer, the One to whom all
   the nations will submit and obey (Gen. 49:10;
   Eph. 2:14-15):
   a. The scepter, a symbol of the kingdom
      (Psa. 45:6; Heb. 1:8), denotes the kingly
      authority of Christ; that the scepter will
      never depart from Judah means that the
      kingship will never depart from Christ
      (2 Sam. 7:12-13; Dan. 2:44-45; 7:13-14;
      Rev. 11:15; 22:1, 3); we must be under the
      ruling of Christ to reign for Christ over
      Satan, sin, and death (Col. 2:19; Rom.
      5:17).
   b. *Shiloh,* meaning "peace bringer," refers
      to Christ in His second coming as the
      Prince of Peace, who will bring peace to
      the whole earth (Isa. 9:6-7; 2:4; Rom.
      14:17; Col. 3:15; Matt. 14:22-33; cf. Job
      3:25-26; Prov. 3:25-26).
3. Due to His victory and kingship, Christ can
   be enjoyed by us to be our rest—our perfect
   peace and full satisfaction (Gen. 49:11-12):
   a. To bind our donkey, or our foal, to the vine
      indicates that the journey is over and
      that the destination has been reached;
      the vine in verse 11 typifies the living
      Christ, who is full of life.
   b. To bind our donkey to the vine signifies to
      cease from our labor and our striving in
      our natural life and to rest in Christ, the

living One who is the source of life (John
15:1, 5; Matt. 11:28-30); because Christ
has won the victory and has gained the
kingdom, He has become the rich vine to
us for our enjoyment, rest, and satisfaction.

c. Garments signify our behavior in our
daily living, and wine signifies life (Gen.
49:11b; John 2:3); hence, to wash our garments in wine and our robe in the blood
of grapes signifies to soak our behavior,
our daily walk, in the enjoyment of the
riches of Christ's life (Matt. 9:17 and footnote 1).

d. The eyes being red with wine and the
teeth being white with milk (Gen. 49:12)
signifies transformation from death to
life by the enjoyment of the rich life of
Christ (John 10:10; Judg. 9:13); the whiteness of the teeth indicates the sound,
healthy function to take in God's Word
as food and to utter His word so that
others may be nourished (Eph. 6:19).

Day 5 B. The prophecy concerning Zebulun portrays the
preaching of the gospel (Gen. 49:13):

1. Zebulun, a seaport, was part of Galilee,
the place where the Lord Jesus began His
ministry of the preaching of the gospel of
the kingdom (v. 13; Matt. 4:12-23; 28:7, 10,
16-20).

2. Zebulun typifies Christ as the "shore" of
the evangelists for the transportation and
spreading in the preaching of God's gospel;
after Christ accomplished all the things that
are to be proclaimed as the gospel, on the day
of Pentecost at least one hundred twenty
gospel "ships," all of whom were Galileans
(Acts 2:7; 13:31), set out from the "shore" to
spread the gospel (Deut. 33:18a).

3. We can be the Galilean preachers, the gospel "ships," who sail out from Christ as the "shore" through prayer by the power of the Holy Spirit as the heavenly wind and with the riches of Christ in the Word to reach the whole world (Acts 1:8; 2:2-41; 4:31; Psa. 68:1, 11-13, 18-19, 27).

Day 6   C. The prophecy concerning Issachar portrays the church life (Gen. 49:14):

1. The strong donkey signifies the natural man; to couch is to rest in satisfaction; and the sheepfolds signify the denominations and various religions based on the law (v. 14; cf. John 10:1-9, 16).

2. The poetry in Genesis 49:14 portrays the genuine church life as the issue of the preaching of the gospel, in which our natural man rests in satisfaction between (outside) the religious sheepfolds; the land typifies Christ as the green pasture enjoyed by the believers in the church life (vv. 14-15a; John 10:9).

3. In Moses' blessing in Deuteronomy 33:18b, Issachar was to rejoice for his tents; there the tents signify the local churches as the expressions of the unique Body of Christ (Eph. 4:4a), in which the believers rejoice in the enjoyment of Christ's riches (Phil. 4:4; 1 Thes. 5:16).

4. This enjoyment issues in our willingness to carry out our service, which is assigned by Christ as the Head; such service becomes a tribute offered to the Master for His satisfaction (Gen. 49:15b; 1 Cor. 12:4-6, 18, 28; Eph. 2:10; 4:11-12; cf. Rom. 15:16).

IV. **The consummation concerning Judah (the gospel in the four Gospels), Zebulun (the preaching of the gospel in the Acts), and Issachar (the church life fulfilled in the remaining books of the New Testament) is**

seen in Deuteronomy 33:19, which says that
the peoples, the nations, will be called to the
mountain, signifying the kingdom of God
(Dan. 2:35), where they will offer sacrifices
of righteousness and enjoy the abundance of
the seas (the church composed mainly of Gentile believers—footnote on Matt. 13:1) and
the hidden treasures of the sand (the kingdom hidden in the earth—v. 44); this shows
that the gospel, the preaching of the gospel,
and the church life as the issue of the gospel result in the enjoyment of the church life
and the kingdom life (Rom. 14:17).

Morning Nourishment

Gen. **Reuben, you are my firstborn, my might and the**
49:3-4 **firstfruits of my vigor, preeminent in dignity and**
preeminent in power. Ebullient as water, you will
not have the preeminence, because you went up
to your father's bed; then you defiled *it*—**he went**
up to my couch.

Deut. **May Reuben live and not die, nor his men be few.**
33:6

[In] Jacob's prophesying with blessing (Gen. 49:1-28),...
although this word of prophecy was spoken by a man, it was
nonetheless the word of God. Because, in his maturity, Jacob
was one with God, whatever he said was God's word.

According to the record of Genesis, the human race began
with Adam and continued with Abel, Enosh, Enoch, Noah, Abraham, Isaac, and Jacob. Eventually, Jacob was no longer an individual, because he became the father of a house that was chosen
by God. This house, the house of Jacob (46:27), was composed
mainly of Jacob's twelve sons. Later, these twelve sons became
the twelve tribes of the nation of Israel. This indicates that
God's intention is to have a house, not individuals. The house of
Israel was a type of the church, which is God's house today. In
the Old Testament we have a house, the house of Israel, and
in the New Testament we also have a house, the church of the
living God (1 Tim. 3:15). (*Life-study of Genesis*, p. 1243)

Today's Reading

Whatever is spoken regarding the house of Israel is a type, a
picture, and a shadow of the church....Because the church is a spiritual entity, it is difficult for us to understand it. Thus, we need the
picture of the house of Israel in the Old Testament....When we examine the picture in the Old Testament, we are able to understand
many aspects of the church revealed in the New Testament....If we
want to know ourselves, we should look at the photograph of ourselves in these twelve tribes. Do not think that the prophecies in
Genesis 49 are only concerned with the sons of Jacob. These prophecies probably concern us more than they do Jacob's twelve sons.

According to Jacob's prophecy with blessing, it is possible for our natural status and disposition to be changed....Throughout the years, I have been speaking to the elders about their disposition....When the elders ask me how they can be more useful, I always tell them that their usefulness depends upon their disposition. I have often told them that their natural disposition is the main reason they are not useful....But...in Genesis 49 there is some good news for those who have been disappointed about their natural disposition. In this group,...[Reuben, Simeon, and Levi], we see not only that our natural status may be changed but also that our natural disposition can be used by God...[yet] only if certain conditions are met.

Reuben lost the preeminence of the birthright because of one sin....For the Lord's name, for the church's testimony, for your protection, and for the honor of your physical body, you must follow this principle of not being alone with a member of the opposite sex. If you follow this principle, you will be preserved.

Joseph received the birthright because he fled from the very defilement that Reuben indulged in (39:7-12). Joseph did not go in the house purposely to be with Potiphar's wife. He was a servant working in the house, and she tempted him. Joseph fled from this temptation. Whenever this temptation comes, the only way to deal with it is to flee. Do not talk or reason with the other party—run away. Reuben lost the birthright because of his defilement, and Joseph obtained it because of his purity. God is righteous, just, and fair. Reuben was on the dark side, and he lost; Joseph was on the bright side, and he gained. Because Reuben was in danger of dying, or at least of being reduced, Moses prayed that he would not die. Anyone in the church life who commits fornication will be in a very dangerous position. He will not only lose the top portion of the enjoyment of Christ; he will be in danger of dying or of being reduced. This is the experience of Reuben. (*Life-study of Genesis,* pp. 1243-1245, 1249-1251)

Further Reading: The God of Abraham, Isaac, and Jacob, chs. 11-12

Enlightenment and inspiration: _____

_____

_____

_____

Morning Nourishment

Gen. Simeon and Levi are brothers; weapons of violence
49:5-7 are their swords. Come not into their council, O my
soul; be not united with their assembly, O my glory;
for in their anger they slew men, and in their self-
will they hamstrung oxen. Cursed be their anger,
for it is fierce; and their wrath, for it is cruel: I will
divide them in Jacob, and scatter them in Israel.

Jacob put Simeon and Levi together in his prophecy because
they were the same in character and disposition. Their disposition was exposed in Genesis 34..., [which] records the defilement
of their sister, Dinah, and their revenge on Hamor and Shechem.
Simeon, Levi, and Dinah were all born of the same mother. Thus,
these brothers dearly loved their sister. When they learned that
she had been defiled, their disposition was exposed by the way
they killed all the males in the city of Shechem, plundered the
city, and even hamstrung the cattle. How cruel they were! The
cruelty of Simeon and Levi terrified Jacob....Nevertheless, in
God's sovereignty, the events in that chapter were a great help to
Jacob's maturity. (Life-study of Genesis, pp. 1245-1246)

Today's Reading

Simeon and Levi received no blessing because of their cruelty (Gen. 34:25-30)....Jacob...would not allow them to dwell
together. Rather, he exercised judgment over them to scatter
them among the children of Israel so that they would not be
able to behave cruelly according to their disposition.

Although Simeon and Levi were companions, Levi eventually
took the opportunity to have his natural disposition changed....
At the time the children of Israel worshipped the golden calf,
Levi's killing disposition was used by God (Exo. 32:29). When
Moses came down from the mountain with the tablets and saw
the people worshipping the golden calf, he said, "Whoever is for
Jehovah, come to me" (Exo. 32:26). Out of all the tribes, only one
tribe, the tribe of Levi, gathered together unto Moses....This indicates that, although we may have a very ugly disposition, our

disposition may still be useful in God's purpose. However, there are certain conditions that must be met. Firstly, we must consecrate ourselves; secondly, we must exercise our disposition against our natural likes and dislikes; and thirdly, we must use our disposition in a renewed, transformed way. Because the inhabitants of the city of Shechem were Levi's enemies, it was easy for him to kill them. But it was quite another matter to kill parents, brothers, sons, and relatives. In order to do this, you must exercise your disposition against your desire and use it in a new way, a way that is both for God and with God....Levi's natural disposition, his slaying disposition, was transformed.

Through transformation work a disposition was not only used by God to kill the idol worshippers but also to slay the sacrifices for offerings to God. Our natural disposition will be useful if three conditions are met: consecration, using it against our natural desire, and using it in a renewed and transformed way. Because Levi's disposition was changed, he became a great blessing. God's Thummim and Urim were with him (Deut. 33:8), and he had the privilege of coming into the presence of God to serve Him. Although the double portion of the land is rich, the privilege of entering God's presence is intimate. The priesthood can be considered as the sweet portion of the birthright. Levi received this portion.

Levi was scattered among the children of Israel. Moses, a God-man, was very happy with Levi. However, he could not annul the prophecy of Jacob; rather, he had to fulfill it. Therefore, the Lord said to Moses, "Command the children of Israel to give to the Levites some of the inheritance of their possession, cities to dwell in; and you shall give to the Levites pasture lands around their cities" (Num. 35:2)....The scattering of Levi according to the curse actually became a blessing. The Levites brought people to God and God to the people. Thus, in ancient times, it was a blessing to have some Levites in your city or in your territory (Judg. 17:7-13). (*Life-study of Genesis,* pp. 1251-1254)

Further Reading: Life-study of Genesis, msg. 98

Enlightenment and inspiration: _____

_____

_____

_____

Morning Nourishment

Gen. Judah, your brothers will praise you; your hand
49:8-9 will be on the neck of your enemies; your father's
sons will bow down before you. Judah is a young
lion; from the prey, my son, you have gone up. He
couches, he stretches out like a lion, and like a lioness; who will rouse him up?

Rev. ...Do not weep; behold, the Lion of the tribe of
5:5 Judah, the Root of David, has overcome...

According to the Old Testament, the twelve sons of Jacob are
arranged in four groups of three....The [first] group of Reuben,
Simeon, and Levi...was utterly evil in the eyes of God....What
a poor beginning it was! However, this should be an encourage-
ment to us because our beginning was also very poor.

The second group is composed of Judah, Zebulun, and Issachar. Because Christ comes in with this group, it is the group of
victory. In this group we have the gospel...signified by Judah
and fully recorded in the four Gospels; the preaching of the
gospel signified by Zebulun and fully recorded in the book of
Acts; and the church life signified by Issachar and fully recorded
in the remaining books of the New Testament beginning with
Romans. The result is the enjoyment of the church life and the
kingdom life. (*Life-study of Genesis,* pp. 1285, 1296)

Today's Reading

Genesis 49:9 says that Judah is a lion. In Revelation 5:5
Christ is called the Lion of the tribe of Judah. This proves that
Genesis 49 needs Revelation 5 for its development....In the New
Testament there are three main truths concerning Christ.

The first is the truth of the victory of Christ....He has accomplished everything God required of Him....He took care of sin,
solved the problem of the world, defeated Satan, abolished
death, and eliminated every negative thing. He has gained the
full victory for the accomplishment of God's purpose.

The second main truth is the truth of the authority of Christ,
the kingdom of Christ. Because Christ has won the victory,

He has been made Lord of all. All authority in heaven and on earth has been given to Him (Matt. 28:18). Furthermore, He has received the universal and eternal kingdom of His Father. Thus, He has the authority, the kingship, and the kingdom.

The third main truth in the New Testament concerning Christ is the truth of the enjoyment and rest in Christ. Christ has accomplished everything in His victory and He has received the authority and the kingdom so that we may have enjoyment and find rest in Him....These three truths are a summary of the New Testament.

In his prophecy Jacob likened Judah to a lion in three aspects: a young lion, a couching lion, and a lioness. The young lion is for fighting, for seizing the prey....The words "you have gone up" [Gen. 49:9] imply that the young lion first had to come down. He came down from the mountain to the plain to capture his prey. After the young lion seized his prey, he went up to the mountaintop again to enjoy it. When Christ was on earth and was crucified on the cross, He was a young lion seizing the prey. And what a prey He captured! It included the whole world, all the sinners, and even Satan, the serpent. From seizing His prey Christ has gone up to the mountaintop, that is, to the third heaven....Ephesians 4:8 says that when Christ ascended to the height, He led captive those taken captive. Christ gained the victory; He put His hand upon Satan's neck....As the young lion, He has overcome all His enemies.

After a lion has enjoyed his prey and has been satisfied, he couches; he lies down to rest in satisfaction. The figure of the couching lion in Genesis 49:9 describes Christ as the One enjoying His rest in the heavens. After gaining the victory and enjoying the prey, He was satisfied....This rest and satisfaction are the issue of Christ's victory. Christ is no longer fighting; rather, He is couching.

Christ is also likened to a lioness [v. 9]. As a lioness, He has produced many cubs. We all are Christ's cubs....Toward men we are lambs following the Lamb; but toward Satan we are lion cubs. (*Life-study of Genesis,* pp. 1273-1275)

Further Reading: Life-study of Genesis, msg. 100

Enlightenment and inspiration: _____

_____

_____

_____

Morning Nourishment

Gen. **The scepter will not depart from Judah, nor the**
49:10-12 **ruler's staff from between his feet, until Shiloh comes,**
and to Him shall be the obedience of the peoples.
Binding his foal to the vine, and his donkey's colt
to the choice vine, he washes his garment in wine,
and his robe in the blood of grapes. Dark are his
eyes with wine, and white are his teeth with milk.

The scepter in Genesis 49:10 denotes the scepter of the
kingship or of the kingdom. Psalm 45:6 says, "The scepter of
uprightness is the scepter of Your kingdom." The scepter,
a symbol of the kingdom, refers to the kingly authority of
Christ....For the scepter never to depart from Judah means
the kingship will never depart from Christ.

[In Genesis 49:10], the word *Shiloh* means "peace bringer."
Most good Bible teachers agree that Shiloh refers to Christ in
His second coming. When Christ comes the second time, He
will come as the Prince of Peace, as the One who brings peace.
At that time, the whole earth will be filled with peace.

The peoples in verse 10 are equivalent to the nations. At the
second coming of Christ, all nations will submit to Him and
obey Him. Isaiah 2:1 through 3 and 11:10 indicate that from
the beginning of the millennium at the Lord's second coming,
all nations will obey Christ. They will come to Him to receive
God's instructions. (*Life-study of Genesis,* pp. 1263-1264)

Today's Reading

Genesis 49:11 says, "Binding his foal to the vine, / And his donkey's colt to the choice vine." We all must bind our donkey to the
vine. I hope that this saying will become a proverb among us....
When the Lord Jesus entered Jerusalem shortly before His crucifixion, He also rode upon a donkey (Matt. 21:5). According to the
Bible, a donkey is always used for traveling toward a goal. To tie a
donkey to something indicates that the journey is over, that you
have arrived at your destination, and that you have reached your
goal. To bind a donkey is not a negative thing. Any donkey would

be happy to be bound to a vine. A donkey's labor is to travel to a certain destination with a certain goal....Without one exception, all Christians are also journeying, striving, and laboring donkeys....Our destination is the vine, the living Christ who is full of life. We must bind our donkey to this vine. This means that we must cease our labor and our striving and rest in Christ, the living One....It is through His victory that He can be the vine.

[Genesis 49:11 speaks of washing] our garments in wine and our robe in the blood of grapes....Figuratively speaking, garments or clothes signify our behavior. They represent our walk and acts. Hence, to wash our garments in wine and our robe in the blood of grapes signifies that we soak our behavior, our daily walk, in the enjoyment of the riches of Christ's life.

Through resting in the enjoyment of Christ's riches in life, we are transformed. Verse 12 says, "Dark are his eyes with wine, / And white are his teeth with milk." This signifies transformation by the rich life of Christ. When we are transformed in this way, our appearance is changed. Those who suffer from famine have a gray color around their eyes. Because they lack adequate nourishment, they are short of the blood supply to their eyes. But we, the kingdom people who enjoy Christ, are never undernourished. On the contrary, we are so fully nourished that our eyes become red. This indicates that we have been transformed from death to life....According to verse 12, the eyes are dark (or, red) with wine. This redness does not come from outward coloring or painting but from the inward, energizing wine.

Verse 12 also speaks of teeth that are white with milk. Our teeth have two functions. The first is to eat, to receive food into the mouth; the second is to help our utterance. The whiteness of the teeth here indicates the sound, healthy function of the teeth. Because I have received the proper nourishment, I have healthy, white teeth to take in God's Word as food and to utter His Word that others may be nourished. (*Life-study of Genesis,* pp. 1279-1284)

Further Reading: Life-study of Genesis, msg. 99

Enlightenment and inspiration: _____

_____

_____

_____

Morning Nourishment

Gen. Zebulun will dwell at the shore of the sea, and he will
49:13 be a shore for ships, and his flank will be toward
Sidon.
Matt. "Land of Zebulun and land of Naphtali, the way to
4:15 the sea, beyond the Jordan, Galilee of the Gentiles."
Deut. ...Rejoice, Zebulun, for your going forth...
33:18

Matthew 4:15 indicates that Zebulun was part of Galilee.
The Lord Jesus began His ministry of the preaching of the
gospel of the kingdom from Galilee. After His resurrection, the
angel charged the women to tell the disciples, "Behold, He goes
before you into Galilee. There you will see Him" (Matt. 28:7).
There in Galilee the resurrected Christ met with the disciples
and charged them to preach the gospel. The disciples "went to
Galilee, to the mountain where Jesus directed them," and it was
there He said to them, "Go therefore and disciple all the nations"
(Matt. 28:16, 19)....Acts 1:11 reveals that the first preachers
of the gospel were men of Galilee....Judah is the tribe producing the gospel. After the gospel is produced, there is the need
for the preaching of the gospel. Therefore, Zebulun comes in to
carry out this mission, to discharge the burden of sending forth
the gospel. (*Life-study of Genesis,* pp. 1288-1289)

Today's Reading

The proper way is to export the gospel by sailing ships
empowered by the heavenly wind. In Acts 1:8 the Lord told the
Galilean preachers to wait until they had received the power
from on high, and Acts 2:2 says, "And suddenly there was a
sound out of heaven, as of a rushing violent wind." From that time
onward, the ships began to sail. One of these living ships was
named Peter. On the day of Pentecost, Peter was not a donkey
journeying and laboring, telling others that Jesus was the
Savior and they had to believe in Him or else they would perish.
He was a ship sailing by the power of a rushing mighty wind.

The gospel goes out by sailing ships, not by steam ships
powered by man-made engines. Do not use any gimmicks in the

preaching of the gospel. To preach the gospel by means of gimmicks is to change the sailing ship into a steamer....According to church history, whenever the gospel has been carried out, it has been carried out by sailing boats, by saints who sailed like ships under the power of the heavenly wind....According to spiritual history, the book of Acts follows the four Gospels, and the Acts is the book of the Galilean preachers. These Galilean preachers were ships sailing by the power of the heavenly wind.

Sidon was a heathen city outside the Holy Land. It was located on the sea, and from it the sea traffic went to the uttermost parts of the earth....In Acts the early preachers sailed from the Holy Land to Asia Minor and then across the Aegean Sea to Greece, Rome, and Spain. The apostle Paul took a ship from the Holy Land and sailed firstly to Sidon and eventually to Rome (Acts 27:3; 28:14). Therefore, Genesis 49:13 was fulfilled in the history of the gospel preaching recorded in Acts.

In the record of Judah the significant word is *lion,* and in the record of Zebulun the significant word is *ships.* The lion is singular, whereas the ships are plural. There is just one Christ, but many Galilean preachers. There is one gospel, but many ships. The church in Anaheim is a haven of ships. We are ships in the haven being prepared to sail out with Christ as the gospel. Young people, are you not Galilean ships ready to sail out? As ships, you must be ready to sail. But do not sail forth to start a movement.

The going forth mentioned in Deuteronomy 33:18 refers to the shipping out. Thus, the word of Moses corresponds to the word of Jacob. Jacob likened Zebulun to ships, which, of course, are for going out, and Moses told Zebulun to rejoice in his going out. If we go out for the preaching of the gospel, we shall rejoice. The person most full of rejoicing and happiness is the gospel preacher. If you are a ship sailing by the power of the heavenly wind, you will be happy, rejoicing, and beside yourself with joy. (*Life-study of Genesis,* pp. 1289-1291)

Further Reading: Life-study of Genesis, msg. 101

Enlightenment and inspiration: _____

_____

_____

_____

Morning Nourishment

Gen. Issachar is a strong donkey, couching between the
49:14-15 sheepfolds. And he saw a resting place that was
good and the land that was pleasant, and he bowed
his shoulder to bear, and became a task-worker...

Deut. They shall call peoples to the mountain; there they
33:19 shall offer sacrifices of righteousness; for they shall
suck the abundance of the seas and the hidden
treasures of the sand.

It is important that Issachar does not precede Zebulun.
What is the spiritual significance of Issachar?...After the four
Gospels and the Acts, we have the Epistles, which cover the
matter of the church life. Therefore, Issachar signifies and represents the church life. (*Life-study of Genesis*, pp. 1291-1292)

Today's Reading

[Issachar's being] likened to a strong donkey couching between
the sheepfolds (Gen. 49:14)...connects verse 14 with verse 11, which
speaks of binding the young donkey to the vine. Thus, the donkey
links Issachar to Judah. In Judah, in the gospel, we have the young
donkey bound to Christ the vine. In Issachar, in the church life, we
have the strong donkey couching between the sheepfolds. In Genesis 49 couching means resting in satisfaction....In Judah we are
young donkeys, but here in Issachar we are strong donkeys. These
strong donkeys are neither laboring nor journeying, but couching.

Notice that this couching donkey is not resting in the sheepfolds; rather, he is resting between the sheepfolds. Every denomi-
nation and religion is a fold. Today, we are not resting in any denominational fold. Instead, we are resting outside the folds....The
Lord made it clear that Judaism was a fold holding God's flock and
that He came into this fold for the purpose of leading the flock out
of it [John 10:16]....Although Issachar is not very far from the folds,
he is not in any of them. This is exactly our situation today.

You may be wondering how a donkey could be among the
sheepfolds. In a sense, we all are sheep of the flock. But according
to our natural man, we all are donkeys....According to our nature,

none of us is a sheep....Nevertheless, we are also the transformed ones....By origin, I was a donkey. But by regeneration I am now a sheep resting among the denominations. Thus, we are a flock of transformed donkeys resting between the sheepfolds.

As we are resting in the church life, [ceasing from our labor and resting in Christ (Matt. 11:28)] among the denominational folds, we enjoy the good rest and the rich pleasant land [Gen. 49:15]. This land is Christ...as our green pasture.

As we rest in the church life, couching between the denominations, realizing the rest, and enjoying the pleasant land, we are willing to lower our shoulder to serve and to bear some responsibility [v. 15]. We become a task-worker. Taskwork...is not our chosen work but the work assigned by the Lord. It is the task assigned by the Head to us as members of the Body. Whatever we do as an assigned portion of the Body service is taskwork. Eventually this taskwork becomes a tribute offered to our Master,...something to offer...for [His] satisfaction.

After the producing of the gospel, the preaching of the gospel, and the issue of the preaching of the gospel, the church life, we come to the consummation, which is found in Deuteronomy 33:19....Firstly, in the consummation the peoples are invited to the mountain of God. In the church life today we are inviting others to the mountain of God, that is, to the kingdom of God....Secondly, on the mountain the peoples will offer sacrifices of righteousness to God...(1 Pet. 2:5; Heb. 13:15-16; Phil. 4:18)....Thirdly, the church and the kingdom become our enjoyment... signified by..."the abundance of the seas and hidden treasures of the sand" [Deut. 33:19]....In Matthew 13, the treasure refers to the kingdom, and the pearl refers to the church. I believe the abundance of the seas...is the church. Undoubtedly, the seas signify the nations....Out of the Gentile world the church is brought forth as the abundance....The kingdom is the treasure hid in the sand, or hid in the earth. (*Life-study of Genesis,* pp. 1292-1296)

Further Reading: Life-study of Genesis, msg. 101

Enlightenment and inspiration: _____

_____

_____

_____

Hymns, #1272

1   The birthright God has giv'n to us
    Must be our goal, our highest prize,
    For we're the church of the first-born —
    Let us our portion realize!

2   A double portion of the land
    Was Joseph's birthright — and 'tis ours
    If we our garments keep from sin,
    And stay pure in temptation's hour.

3   The priesthood was to Levi giv'n
    As his inheritance — for he
    Did count his family ties but loss
    And owned God's things supreme to be.

4   The kingship, Judah did receive
    For tending to young Joseph's need;
    Through Benjamin's adversity,
    He was his comforter indeed.

5   The double portion we would seek,
    The priesthood and the kingship too;
    Make us so desperate, Lord, for Thee
    That Thee, our birthright, we'd pursue.

6   We would be those who pay the price,
    Deny the soul, reject the self;
    Ambitious for the birthright thus
    We'd gain Thee, Lord, above all else.

7   The promise, Lord, 'twas giv'n to us,
    Oh, let us ne'er this right despise;
    Enflame us, Lord, to gain Thyself,
    And Thee, our birthright realize.

Composition for prophecy with main point and sub-points: _____

Jacob's Prophesying with Blessing
(2)

Scripture Reading: Gen. 49:16-28

Day 1   I. **The prophecy concerning the apostasy with Dan indicates Jacob's concern about the setting up of a divisive center of worship (Gen. 49:16-18; Judg. 17:9-10; 18:27-31; 1 Kings 12:26-31):**

A. Dan fought as a young lion to gain more land (signifying Christ), but after being successful and victorious, he became a serpent—proud, individualistic, and independent; he acted in his pride to set up an idol and a divisive center of worship and to ordain a hired priest in the city of Dan during the time that the house of God was in Shiloh (Deut. 33:22; Josh. 19:47; Judg. 18:27-31; cf. Deut. 12:5).

B. As a serpent, Dan bit the horse's heels so that its rider fell backward (Gen. 49:17), signifying that the apostasy brought in by Dan became a great stumbling block to the nation of Israel; throughout the history of the church many spiritual people have followed Dan's example, thereby frustrating God's people from going on in His ordained way; a further fulfillment of Jacob's prophecy concerning Dan is seen in 1 Kings 12:26-31.

C. The source of Dan's apostasy was in not caring for his brothers; not caring for the other parts of the Body is the source of apostasy, resulting in competition (v. 31).

D. Division is not only denominationalism but can also involve localism and regionalism; even in our personal experience we can be distracted from the right way in following God and actually be working for our self-interest:

1. The best way to be safeguarded from falling into apostasy is by taking care of others to care for the entire Body and the Lord's unique testimony in the Lord's one work; if Dan had consulted the other tribes, he would have been kept from apostasy (cf. 1 Cor. 12:20; 15:58; 16:10; Acts 15:1-2).

2. We can be healed from our apostasy and enjoy the Lord's boundless love by returning to the Lord, acknowledging our offense to Him to be forgiven of all our iniquity, seeking His face, and pursuing to know Him so that we may live in His presence, in resurrection (Hosea 5:13—6:3; 14:1-8).

Day 2   II. **The prophecy concerning the recovery with Gad indicates not only his victory but also that he would not enjoy his victory by himself (Gen. 49:19; Deut. 33:20-21):**

A. Gad's victory, corresponding to his victory in Deuteronomy 33:20, signifies the recovery of the victory of Christ lost by Dan because of his apostasy.

B. Gad provided the first part of the good land (the land east of the Jordan) for himself, but before enjoying his portion, he fought with his brothers to gain their portion of the land west of the Jordan, thus executing Jehovah's righteousness and His judgments in Israel (vv. 20-21; Num. 32:1-32).

C. Dan's failure was because he was individualistic and cared only for himself, whereas Gad's success was because he was corporate and took care of the need of his brothers.

D. In New Testament terms, to follow Gad's example we need to take care of the Body corporately; today this is to be filled with the corporate sense of the Body and to care for the members of the Body for the accomplishing of God's will, which is to have the Body life (Rom. 12).

Day 3   III. **The prophecy concerning the sufficiency of Asher typifies the enjoyment of Christ as the rich provision of life for fighting and building (Gen. 49:20):**

A. Jacob's prophecy in Genesis 49:20 and Moses' blessing in Deuteronomy 33:24-25 show the sufficiency of Asher, coming after the recovery with Gad; Asher was blessed with rich food, with the rich provision of life.

B. Just as Asher was the one "dipping his foot in oil," we can "walk in oil" by enjoying the bountiful supply of the Spirit of Jesus Christ for our daily walk (v. 24; Phil. 1:19; Gal. 3:5; 5:25).

C. When we enjoy the Lord daily as our rich provision of life ("as your days are, so shall your strength be"—Deut. 33:25b), He becomes our secret of sufficiency for us to be content in any situation (Phil. 4:11-13; Psa. 23:1).

D. The issue of such a rich provision is the enjoyment of absolute rest with peace, strength, security, and sufficiency.

Day 4   IV. **The prophecy concerning the consummation with Naphtali typifies that when we experience Christ in resurrection, we become those who will take the earth by preaching Christ as the gospel of the kingdom to the whole inhabited earth (Gen. 49:21; Deut. 33:23; Psa. 22:27; Matt. 28:19; Acts 1:8; Rom. 15:19; Matt. 24:14):**

A. "Naphtali is a hind let loose; / He gives beautiful words" (Gen. 49:21):

1. The hind typifies the resurrected Christ; "the hind of the dawn" (Psa. 22, title) signifies Christ in His resurrection, which took place at early dawn (Luke 24:1).

2. A hind is a deer known for its leaping and jumping; Christ in resurrection is the leaping One (S. S. 2:8-9).

3. Beautiful words, rich and pleasant words, words of joy and life, come out of the experience of the resurrected Christ (Gen. 49:21; Matt. 28:16, 18-20; John 7:37-39a; Acts 2:32-36; 5:20).

B. "O Naphtali, satisfied with favor, / And full of the blessing of Jehovah: / Possess the sea and the south" (Deut. 33:23):

1. Naphtali is satisfied with favor (the Old Testament equivalent of New Testament grace) and is full of the blessing of Jehovah; the blessing does not refer to material blessing but to the blessing in the spirit, the blessing in life, the blessing in the heavenlies (Eph. 1:3).

2. Naphtali will possess the sea (the Gentile world—Matt. 13:1; Dan. 7:3; Rev. 17:15) and the south (the land of Israel), signifying that those who experience the resurrected Christ will possess the whole earth through their proclaiming of Christ (Matt. 28:19; Acts 1:8; Rom. 15:19).

Day 5 V. **The prophecy concerning the universal blessing of the Triune God being with Joseph was due to his being separate from his brothers in the principle of a Nazarite (Gen. 49:22-26; Num. 6:1-9):**

A. Joseph as a fruitful bough by a fountain with branches running over the wall typifies Christ as the branch (Isa. 11:1) for the branching out of God through His believers as His branches (John 15:1, 5), with God as the source of their fruitfulness, to spread Christ over every restriction and limitation, magnifying Him in all circumstances (Gen. 49:22; Phil. 1:20; Acts 4:31).

B. As the one universally blessed by his father, Joseph typifies Christ, the appointed Heir of all things, and Christ's believers, His partners, who participate in His inheritance and who are

blessed by the Father with every spiritual blessing (1 Cor. 3:21-22; Rom. 8:17; Heb. 1:2, 9, 14; 3:14;
Eph. 1:3):

1. The blessings bestowed on Joseph encompass
all time, from ancient times to eternity (Gen.
49:25-26; Deut. 33:13-16), and all space, from
heaven to earth, including the deep under
the earth (Gen. 49:25b; Deut. 33:13-14, 16a);
time plus space equals the universe.

2. The universal blessing on Joseph will consummate in the new heaven and new earth,
in which everything will be new as a blessing to Christ and His believers (Rev. 21:1, 4-5;
22:3, 5):

a. Only God is new; anything that is kept
away from God is old, but anything that
comes back to God is new (2 Cor. 5:17).

b. To be renewed means to come back to
God and have something of God put
into us so that we are mingled with God
and one with God; the secret of receiving God as our blessing of newness is to
bring everything to God and let Him get
into everything (4:16).

c. The universal blessing on Joseph means
that blessing is everywhere; our praises
turn everything of the curse of the fall
into a blessing (cf. Eph. 5:20).

C. Joseph overcame in his sufferings because he
was strengthened by God, the Mighty One of Jacob
and the All-sufficient One, and because he saw
that everything was arranged by God to be a
blessing to him (Gen. 49:24-25; 45:5; 50:20; 1 Cor.
3:21-22; Rom. 8:28; Eph. 5:20; 1 Thes. 5:18).

D. Joseph was blessed with "the favor of Him who
dwelt in the thornbush" (Deut. 33:16a; Exo. 3:2-6,
14-15; Mark 12:26-27); the highest blessing is to
enter into God's dwelling place and stay in His
presence (Psa. 27:4, 8; 84:10-12).

Day 6 VI. **The prophecy concerning the dwelling place of the Triune God being with Benjamin will ultimately consummate in the New Jerusalem as the mutual dwelling of God and His redeemed for eternity; this is the greatest blessing to God's people (Gen. 49:27; Deut. 33:12; Rev. 21:3, 22):**

A. As a tearing wolf, Benjamin is a type of Christ, who destroys the enemy by tearing him to pieces (Gen. 49:27; Eph. 4:8; 2 Cor. 10:5).

B. Moses' blessing of Benjamin says that he will dwell securely beside Jehovah and that Jehovah will dwell between Benjamin's shoulders; Jerusalem with God's temple, God's dwelling place, was located in the territory of Benjamin (Deut. 33:12; Judg. 1:21).

C. All the blessings issue in God's dwelling place; this is God's good pleasure, the desire of His heart (cf. Heb. 11:21; Prov. 4:18; Psa. 90:1; John 15:4; 14:23; Isa. 66:1-2).

VII. **Genesis 49:1-28 is an abstract of the entire Bible and a summary of the history of God's people, as seen in the twelve sons of Jacob, the nation of Israel, and the church; it is also a portrait of the personal history of every believer:**

A. Jacob's first four sons—Reuben, Simeon, Levi, and Judah—were sinners, indicating that the history of God's people begins with sinners; however, two of these sinners, Levi and Judah, were transformed to become priests and kings.

B. Out of the kingship with Judah a kingly salvation was produced, which was preached as the gospel in the Gentile world by Zebulun and which issued in the church life with Issachar; but the apostasy came in through Dan, followed by the recovery with Gad, which issued in the sufficiency of the riches of Christ with Asher and in the resurrection with Naphtali.

C. Finally, the history of God's people concludes with Joseph and Benjamin, who typify Christ as the One who is altogether victorious and perfect, without defect; according to Jacob's prophecy and Moses' word, Joseph brought in God's boundless, universal blessing (vv. 22-26; Deut. 33:13-16), and Benjamin, God's eternal dwelling place (v. 12).

D. Thus, the conclusion of Genesis 49 corresponds with the conclusion of the entire Bible—the universal blessing in the new heaven and the new earth, in which is God's eternal dwelling, the New Jerusalem, as the issue and goal of God's universal blessing (cf. Eph. 1:3; 2:22).

Morning Nourishment

Gen. Dan will judge his people, as one of the tribes of Israel.
49:16-18 Dan will be a serpent in the way, a viper on the path,
that bites the horse's heels, so that his rider falls backward. I have waited for Your salvation, O Jehovah.
Deut. And concerning Dan he said, Dan is a lion's whelp
33:22 that leaps forth from Bashan.

Dan was the continuation of Judah, for Judah was a lion and
Dan was a young lion. As the continuation of Judah, Dan was
successful in gaining more Christ by his victorious life (Deut.
33:22; Josh. 19:47; Judg. 18:27-29).

Because Dan was successful and victorious, he became proud,
individualistic, and independent. He cared only for himself, not
for others. (*Life-study of Genesis,* p. 1317)

Today's Reading

Dan's apostasy was the setting up of a divisive center of worship (Judg. 18:30-31; 17:9-10; 1 Kings 12:26-31; 2 Kings 10:29)....
[Nothing] was more sinful or more damaging to God's people
than Dan's act of setting up a divisive center of worship. In Deuteronomy 12, 14, 15, and 16 the Lord through Moses charged the
children of Israel at least fifteen times not to offer their burnt
offerings in the place of their choice. They were commanded to
go to the unique place the Lord had chosen for His name and
for His habitation...[to keep God's] people in oneness.

After the children of Israel entered the good land, the taberna-
cle, the house of God, was in Shiloh (Judg. 18:31). As long as the tab-
ernacle was in Shiloh, Shiloh was the unique center for the worship of God. As the unique center, it should have maintained the
unity of God's people. However, Dan set up another center in the
north, which caused the first division among the children of Israel.

Judges 18:30 says, "The children of Dan set up for themselves the graven image" (Heb.). Here we see that the Danites
did something for themselves. They did not care for the other
tribes. Thus, the source of their apostasy was not caring for
their brothers. Not caring for the other parts of the Body is the

source of apostasy. This apostasy crept in under the guise of the worship of God. The principle is the same today. Many Christians set up other centers, not for gambling or dancing, but for worshipping God. Although this seems so positive, it is actually done by the self and for the self. Every divisive center is established for someone's self-interest. Such a practice causes not only division but also competition.

Dan did not care for the other tribes; he cared only for his own tribe. After he won the victory and gained the expansion, the enlargement, he did something for himself. This was the source of his apostasy. According to the Old Testament, the Lord never forgot Dan's apostasy. In the eyes of God it was the worst sin in His economy....Nothing is more destructive than division among God's people. Divisive worship centers are often related to idols. Because the devil lurks behind idols, by setting up an idol Dan became a serpent. Whenever you become divisive, no matter how good your reason may be, there will be something behind you— the serpent, the subtle one....Whenever you do not care for others, but only for your interests, doing something merely for yourself, the serpent is at hand. The best way to be safeguarded from falling into apostasy is taking care of others....If Dan had consulted the other tribes, he would have been kept from apostasy.

Dan not only set up a divisive center, but also ordained the hired "priests" (Judg. 18:30; 1 Kings 12:31). To hire the common people to be priests was profane because it destroyed God's holy ordination. In the downfall of the church, many unsaved ones have been hired to do the service of God. This is apostasy. In God's New Testament economy, all true believers are made priests of God (1 Pet. 2:9; Rev. 1:6; 5:10). But degraded Christianity has built up a system to ordain some of the believers to do the service of God, making them a clerical hierarchy and leaving the rest of the believers as laymen. This also is a form of apostasy. (*Life-study of Genesis*, pp. 1317-1319, 1322-1323)

Further Reading: Life-study of Genesis, msg. 102

Enlightenment and inspiration: _____

_____

_____

_____

Morning Nourishment

Deut. And concerning Gad he said, Blessed be He who en-
33:20-21 larges Gad. He dwells as a lioness, and tears off the
arm, yea, even the top of the head. And he provided
the first part for himself, for there the portion of
a lawgiver is reserved; and he came with the heads
of the people; he executed the righteousness of
Jehovah and His judgments with Israel.

With Gad we see recovery. After the apostasy of Dan, Gad came
in to recover the lost victory (Gen. 49:19). The victory of Judah, the
lion, had been lost by Dan's apostasy, but Gad regained it and
even enlarged it. Gad is not a young lion but a lioness producing
cubs. He is the continuation of the victorious Judah and Dan.

God was so happy about Gad's recovery of the victory that He enlarged him [Deut. 33:20]....Gad was enlarged not only by God, but
also for God. He was enlarged for the executing of God's righteousness among God's people. (*Life-study of Genesis,* pp. 1323-1324)

Today's Reading

The best aspect of Gad is not merely that he crushed the
enemy's head but that he would not enjoy his victory by himself.
Although he gained land on the east of the Jordan, he would not
enjoy it until the other tribes had won their portion of the land. Gad
went with the other tribes to fight the battle to gain more land so
that all the tribes might be able to have their share. The New Testament interpretation of this Old Testament figure is that we must
always take care of the brothers, the members of the Body.

For many years I could not understand Moses' word in Deuteronomy 33:21. This verse says, "And he provided the first part
for himself, / For there the portion of a lawgiver is reserved; / And
he came with the heads of the people; / He executed the righteousness of Jehovah / And His judgments with Israel." Although
I studied this verse again and again, especially the last part about
the heads of the people, I simply could not understand it. But
today I understand this verse. The *first part* refers to the land
east of the Jordan. Gad provided that part for himself; yet he

would not remain there to enjoy it. Instead, he came with the heads of the people, the princes of the other tribes, to fight the battle for the rest of the land. Here we see the action, the move, of the Body. Dan took care of himself individualistically, but Gad took care of the Body corporately. In the church today we would say that Gad was filled with the sense of the Body.

The reason for Gad's success was that he let go of his own enjoyment in order to take care of the Body. This is righteousness in the eyes of God. It is the executing of the righteousness of Jehovah. In New Testament terms, it is the accomplishment of God's will. When the children of Israel entered the good land, it was God's will in His righteousness that His people be settled. God did not want only Gad; He wanted all the twelve tribes to be settled to become His kingdom that His judgments may be observed. This is to accomplish the will of God. Romans 12:1 and 2 say that if we present our bodies a living sacrifice, we shall be able to prove what the will of God is. According to Romans 12, the will of God is simply to have the Body life. Thus, to have the Body life, to take care of the needs of others, is to execute God's righteousness for observing His judgments. Nothing is so right as caring for the members of the Body. No judgments can be observed without the execution of God's righteousness. God's New Testament judgments can only be observed in the Body of Christ, which is built up by the mutual care of its members in righteousness.

Dan's failure was that he was individualistic. Gad's success was that he was corporate, moving with the brothers. Dan was for himself, but Gad was for all the tribes. Whenever you are concerned only for your own spiritual interests, you are a Dan. But when you forget your own spiritual interests and care for all the other brothers, that is, care for the Body, you are a Gad. We must care for the Body and move with the Body. Are you a Dan or a Gad? Are you taking care only of your locality or of the whole Body? As long as we do not care for the Body, we are today's Dan, and we have fallen into a form of apostasy. (*Life-study of Genesis,* pp. 1324-1325)

Further Reading: Life-study of Genesis, msg. 103

Enlightenment and inspiration: _____

_____

_____

_____

Morning Nourishment

Gen. 49:20   Asher's food will be rich, and he will yield royal dainties.

Deut. 33:24-25   And concerning Asher he said, Blessed be Asher above the sons. May he be the one favored of his brothers, and the one dipping his foot in oil. Your doorbolts shall be iron and copper; and as your days are, so shall your strength be.

When we have the victory of Christ and help our brothers gain their portion before we enjoy our own, we have rich food. This rich food even becomes royal dainties, the royal food [Gen. 49:20]. It is not food for the common people, but food for kings, for the royal family....We are not only a lion family but also a royal family. We are a kingly family, and our dining is royal. Whatever we feed on in these life-study messages is royal dainties. (*Life-study of Genesis,* pp. 1309-1310)

Today's Reading

After the recovery with Gad, we have the sufficiency of Asher. The account of Asher begins with the exceeding blessing and the surpassing grace....[In Deuteronomy 33:24] Asher received the exceeding blessing and the foremost grace. Many of us are able to understand this language. In Dan's apostasy we lost all the blessing and the grace, but in Gad's victory the blessing was recovered and the grace was returned. Now in Asher we are enjoying the exceeding blessing and the surpassing grace.

In Asher we also see the rich provision of life. Firstly, Asher has the rich provision for living and growing. Genesis 49:20 says, "Asher's food will be rich, and he will yield royal dainties." Deuteronomy 33:25 indicates that Asher also has the rich provision of life for fighting and building. The first part of this verse says, "Your doorbolts shall be iron and copper." The rich food and royal dainties are for Asher's living and growing, and the iron and copper are minerals for fighting and building. Asher certainly received the richest provision.

Asher also has the bountiful supply of the Spirit for his daily walk (Gal. 5:25). Deuteronomy 33:24 says, "The one dipping his foot in oil." This certainly is figurative speech. The spiritual significance of dipping the foot in oil is being full of the Spirit. In typology oil refers to the Spirit of God. Asher does not have a mere trickle of oil but enough to dip his feet in. This means that in Asher we have the rich, bountiful supply of the Spirit (Phil. 1:19). Oh, we can walk in oil! A number of times in the Lord's recovery I have had the sense that we are walking in oil. I worship, thank, and praise the Lord, saying, "Lord, this is too rich! The supply of the Spirit here is too rich! Our oil is so bountiful!" Do you have oil in which to dip your feet? We do. We have the rich food, the royal dainties, and the rich, bountiful oil in which to dip our feet.

Deuteronomy 33:25 says of Asher, "As your days are, so shall your strength be." When we have the exceeding blessing and surpassing grace, the rich provision of life, and the bountiful supply of the Spirit, we have absolute rest with peace, strength, security, and sufficiency. This was the experience of the apostle Paul in Philippians 4:11-13. He was content in any situation. I can testify that this week I have had the deep sense that I am walking in oil and that I have satisfaction, peace, and rest. I have also been full of strength. Thus, I have security and sufficiency. The Lord is my Shepherd, and I have no want, shortage, or lack (Psa. 23:1). Instead of want, I am full of sufficiency. I have rich food, royal dainties, deep oil, and doorbolts of iron and copper. Everywhere there is provision. Hence, I am safe and secure, and I have rest and strength. Do you have the boldness to say that you have this security and sufficiency? Or would you say that this morning your wife gave you a difficult time and that you barely endured it? You need to be able to say, "This morning my wife gave me a difficult time. But praise the Lord that I walked in deep oil! Now I have rest, peace, security, strength, and sufficiency. My strength is as lasting as my days. As my days, so shall my rest, my security, and my sufficiency be." This is the experience of Asher. (*Life-study of Genesis,* pp. 1326-1327)

Further Reading: Life-study of Genesis, msg. 104

Enlightenment and inspiration: _____

_____

_____

_____

Morning Nourishment

Gen. Naphtali is a hind let loose; he gives beautiful
49:21 words.
Deut. And concerning Naphtali he said, O Naphtali, satis-
33:23 fied with favor, and full of the blessing of Jehovah:
possess the sea and the south.

A hind is a lovely animal, so living and active. Although a
hind is not proud or especially large, it is quite strong, able to
skip upon the mountaintops. According to the Hebrew text,
the title of Psalm 22 speaks of the hind of the dawn,...[which]
signifies the resurrected Christ. Psalm 22 firstly speaks of
Christ's death on the cross. Then, beginning with verse 22, it
proceeds to His resurrection. Psalm 22:22 says, "I will declare
Your name to my brothers; / In the midst of the assembly I will
praise You." This indicates that in His resurrection Christ
declared the name of the Father to His brothers and praised
Him in the midst of the assembly, the church. Thus, this psalm
eventually issues in the resurrection of Christ as the hind of
the dawn. (*Life-study of Genesis*, p. 1328)

Today's Reading

Rich words, pleasant words, beautiful words, words of joy
and life—all these come out of the experience of the resurrected Christ. The more we experience Christ as the resurrected
One, the more we have something to say. We could never be
silent. Everyone who experiences Christ as the resurrected
One will be bubbling over with beautiful words....Christ is the
word of God, the word of life, and the word that is spirit....The
principle here is that we always utter what is filling us within.
The word we speak comes out of the abundance of our inner
being. When our inner being is filled with Christ, we must
speak lest we burst. Now we can understand why Naphtali, a
hind let loose, gives beautiful words. Because he has experienced Christ, he is filled with beautiful words.

[In Deuteronomy 33:23] we see that Naphtali is satisfied
with favor. Favor in the Old Testament is the equivalent of grace

in the New Testament. Thus, Naphtali is satisfied with grace. When we are in resurrection speaking beautiful words, we also are satisfied with grace....This verse also says that Naphtali is filled with the blessing of the Lord. He is satisfied with grace and full of blessing. This is the victorious and matured life in resurrection. As we speak for Christ to nourish others, we ourselves are satisfied with grace and filled with blessing.

The favor and blessing here link Naphtali with Asher, who is more blessed than the sons and favored among his brothers. In the Lord's recovery we are daily satisfied with rich grace and full of God's blessing. This blessing does not refer to the material blessing, but to the blessing in the spirit, the blessing in life, the blessing in the heavenlies. What grace we have tasted and what blessing we have enjoyed since coming into the church life!...(1 Cor. 15:10; 2 Cor. 13:14).

Naphtali will possess the west, the sea, the Gentile world, and the south, the land, the nation of Israel. This means that Naphtali will take the earth. It is the resurrected Christ experienced by us who will take the earth. At the end of Psalm 22 we see that the resurrected Christ will gain the nations. Psalm 22:27 says, "All the ends of the earth / Will remember and return to Jehovah, / And all families of the nations / Will worship before You." All the nations will submit to Him, obey Him, and worship Him....When we truly experience Christ in resurrection, we become those who will take the earth by preaching Christ (Matt. 28:19; Acts 1:8; Rom. 15:19).

In order to take the earth, we must begin from Reuben and continue through Simeon, Levi, Judah, Zebulun, Issachar, Dan, Gad, and Asher until we come to Naphtali. When we have become Naphtali...it is easy to take the earth because we are in resurrection speaking beautiful words, and we are satisfied with favor and full of blessing. (*Life-study of Genesis,* pp. 1329, 1312, 1329-1330, 1313)

Further Reading: Life-study of Genesis, msg. 103

Enlightenment and inspiration: _____

_____

_____

_____

Morning Nourishment

Gen. Joseph is a fruitful bough, a fruitful bough by a
49:22 fountain; *his* branches run over the wall.
25-26 ...From the All-sufficient One, who will bless you
with blessings of heaven above, blessings of the
deep that lies beneath, blessings of the breasts
and of the womb. The blessings of your father surpass the blessings of my ancestors to the utmost
bound of the everlasting hills...

Joseph as a fruitful bough typifies Christ as the branch (Isa.
11:1) for the branching out of God through His believers as His
branches (John 15:1, 5). In Genesis 49:22 the fountain signifies
God, the source of fruitfulness (Psa. 36:9; Jer. 2:13), and the
branches' running over the wall signifies that Christ's believers
as His branches spread Christ over every restriction, magnifying Him in all circumstances (Phil. 1:20; 4:22; Philem. 10). (Gen.
49:22, footnote 1)

The blessings bestowed on Joseph, as seen in Genesis 49:25-26
and Deuteronomy 33:13-16, encompass all time, from ancient
times to eternity (Gen. 49:26; Deut. 33:15), and all space, from
heaven to earth, including the deep under the earth (Gen. 49:25b;
Deut. 33:13-14, 16a). Time plus space equals the universe. As the
one universally blessed by his father, Joseph typifies Christ, the
appointed Heir of all things (Heb. 1:2; Col. 1:16), and His believers, Christ's partners who participate in His inheritance (1 Cor.
3:21-22; Rom. 8:17; Heb. 1:9; 3:14; 1:14 and footnote). The universal blessing on Joseph will consummate in the new heaven and
new earth, in which everything will be a blessing to Christ and His
believers (Rev. 21:1, 4-5; 22:3, 5). (Gen. 49:25, footnote 2)

Today's Reading

When we combine the blessings mentioned in Genesis 49:25-26
with those in Deuteronomy 33:13-16, we see that the blessings bestowed upon Joseph were of ten aspects. First, he was blessed with
the precious things of heaven (Deut. 33:13). Certainly some of the
blessings of the precious things of heaven should include rain and

snow. Second, he was blessed with the dew. Third, he was blessed with the blessing of the deep that lies beneath. This refers to the springs, fountains, and waters underneath the earth. Fourth, he was blessed by the precious fruits brought forth by the sun (Deut. 33:14). After that, as the fifth blessing, he had the blessing of the precious things put forth by the moon. We need both the sun, which typifies Christ, and the moon, which typifies the church. Some fruits are brought forth by Christ, and some precious things are put forth by the church....The sixth blessing Joseph received was the blessing of the best things of the ancient mountains, and the seventh was the precious things of the eternal hills (Deut. 33:15). ...From ancient times to eternity, all of time is included, and from heaven to earth, including the deep under the earth, all of space is included. This indicates that all the good things in the universe have become blessings to Joseph. The eighth blessing includes the precious things of the earth and its fullness (Deut. 33:16). Certainly this must include minerals such as gold and silver. The ninth blessing is...the blessings of the womb...for begetting, and the blessings of the breasts...for nourishing [Gen. 49:25]. These refer to the producing of life. This is the only blessing that is of life. The tenth blessing is "the favor of Him who dwelt in the thornbush" (Deut. 33:16)....The One who dwelt in the bush (Exo. 3:4) will dwell in the temple, in the church, and then in the New Jerusalem. All the bushes will be transformed into precious stones. Formerly, God dwelt among the bushes, but eventually He will dwell among the precious stones in the New Jerusalem.

The Hebrew word rendered "separate" [in Genesis 49:26] is also the word for *Nazarite*....[Joseph] was the first Nazarite in the Bible, separate from his brothers, and Christ became the real Nazarite, separate from all the people...to live wholly for God. This separated One has received the blessing of the whole universe. The universal blessing is bestowed upon the crown of the head of such a Nazarite. (*Life-study of Genesis,* pp. 1336-1338)

Further Reading: Life-study of Genesis, msgs. 104-105

Enlightenment and inspiration: _____
_____
_____
_____

Morning Nourishment

Gen. Benjamin is a ravenous wolf, in the morning devour-
49:27 ing the prey and in the evening dividing the spoil.
Deut. Concerning Benjamin he said, The beloved of Jeho-
33:12 vah shall dwell securely beside Him; *Jehovah* shall
cover over him all the day, and He shall dwell between his shoulders.

In Hebrew the word translated "ravenous" [in Genesis 49:27]
means "to tear into pieces." For years I was troubled by the word
wolf in this verse. Although a lion or a tiger seems positive, a
wolf is not positive. However, Christ is not only the overcoming
lion, but also the tearing wolf. Benjamin, a tearing wolf, is also
a type of Christ. Therefore, the reference to a wolf here is positive, not negative. In the morning he will devour the prey, and
in the evening he will divide the spoil, that is, prepare the spoil
for the next morning's meal. This means that Christ is not only
the overcoming One, but also the tearing One, the One who
eats His enemy. (*Life-study of Genesis*, pp. 1339-1340)

Today's Reading

[In Deuteronomy 33:12] the words *beside Him* indicate that
Benjamin will be the Lord's neighbor. He will dwell next door to the
Lord. Because he will dwell next door to the Lord, he will dwell in
safety....This verse also says that the Lord will cover, overshadow,
Benjamin all day long and even dwell between his shoulders....
Jerusalem was not located in the territory of Judah, but in the ter-
ritory of Benjamin (Judg. 1:21). If you consult a map, you will see
that the territory of Benjamin lies with two shoulders toward the
south and that between these two shoulders of Benjamin was
Jerusalem, where the temple, the Lord's dwelling, was located.

Among the twelve sons of Jacob, the first was a sinner, and
the last became the dwelling of God. In Genesis 3 we all were
sinners, but at the end of the Bible, in Revelation 21 and 22,
we all become Benjamin, the dwelling of God....With Joseph we
see that Christ receives the all-inclusive blessing of the universe, and with Benjamin we see that God is dwelling among

His chosen people. This is the New Jerusalem and the new heaven and new earth. The new heaven and new earth are the sphere in which every blessing is bestowed upon Christ. (*Life-study of Genesis,* pp. 1340-1341)

Moses' blessing in Deuteronomy 33:12 says that Benjamin will dwell securely beside Jehovah and that Jehovah will dwell between Benjamin's shoulders....Thus, the blessing of Jacob's twelve sons ends with God's dwelling place, which ultimately consummates in the New Jerusalem as the mutual dwelling of God and His redeemed for eternity (Rev. 21—22).

Genesis 49:1-28 is an abstract of the entire Bible and a summary of the history of God's people, as seen in the twelve sons of Jacob, the nation of Israel, and the church. It is also a portrait of the personal history of every believer. Jacob's first four sons—Reuben, Simeon, Levi, and Judah—were sinners, indicating that the history of God's people begins with sinners. However, two of these sinners, Levi and Judah, were transformed to become priests and kings. Out of the kingship with Judah a kingly salvation was produced, which was preached as the gospel in the Gentile world by Zebulun and which issued in the church life with Issachar. But the apostasy came in through Dan, followed by the recovery with Gad, which issued in the sufficiency of the riches of Christ with Asher and in the resurrection with Naphtali. Finally, the history of God's people concludes with Joseph and Benjamin, who typify Christ as the One who is altogether victorious and perfect, without defect. According to Jacob's prophecy and Moses' word, Joseph brought in God's boundless, universal blessing (vv. 22-26; Deut. 33:13-16), and Benjamin, God's eternal dwelling place (Deut. 33:12). Thus, the conclusion of Genesis 49 corresponds with the conclusion of the entire Bible—the universal blessing in the new heaven and the new earth, in which is God's eternal dwelling, the New Jerusalem, as the issue and goal of God's universal blessing (cf. Eph. 1:3; 2:22). (Gen. 49:27, footnote 2)

Further Reading: Life-study of Genesis, msgs. 106-108

Enlightenment and inspiration: _____

_____

_____

_____

Hymns, #977

1   Glorious things of thee are spoken,
     Holy city of our God;
  He whose word cannot be broken
     Formed thee for His own abode;
  On the Rock of Ages founded,
     What can shake thy sure repose?
  With salvation's walls surrounded,
     Thou may'st smile at all thy foes.

2   See the streams of living waters,
     Springing from eternal love,
  Well supply thy blessed members,
     And all fear of want remove;
  Who can faint, when such a river
     Ever flows their thirst t' assuage?
  Grace which, like the Lord, the giver,
     Never fails from age to age.

3   Blest constituents of Zion,
     Washed in the Redeemer's blood;
  Jesus, whom their souls rely on,
     Makes them kings and priests to God.
  'Tis His love His people raises
     Over self to reign as kings:
  And as priests, His worthy praises,
     Each his thankful offering brings.

4   Savior, if of Zion's city
     I, through grace, a member am,
  Let the world deride or pity —
     I will glory in Thy name.
  Fading is the worldling's pleasure,
     All his boasted pomp and show;
  Solid joys and lasting treasure
     None but Zion's members know.

Composition for prophecy with main point and sub-points: _____

_____
_____
_____
_____
_____
_____
_____
_____
_____
_____
_____
_____
_____
_____
_____
_____
_____
_____
_____
_____
_____
_____
_____
_____
_____
_____
_____
_____
_____
_____
_____
_____
_____
_____
_____
_____
_____

Image and Dominion—
the Heart of Genesis

Scripture Reading: Gen. 1:26-28; Mark 1:14-15; 2 Cor. 4:3-4; Rom. 8:29; 5:17; Col. 1:13, 15; 3:10-11; Matt. 13:43; Rev. 21:10-11; 22:1, 5

Day 1   I. **The book of Genesis begins and ends with image and dominion (1:26-28):**
A. The subject of Genesis is man bearing the image of God and exercising God's dominion over all things (vv. 26-28):
   1. For God to create man in His image means that God created man with the intention that man would become a duplication of God, the reproduction of God, for His corporate expression (John 12:24; Rom. 8:29; Heb. 2:10; 1 John 3:1-2).
   2. God's intention in giving man dominion was for man to exercise God's authority to deal with the enemy, to recover the earth, and to bring in the kingdom of God; dominion and the kingdom are synonymous (Gen. 1:28; Matt. 6:10, 13b).
   3. We were created for the purpose of expressing God and exercising His dominion; this is the heart of Genesis.
B. Genesis concludes with a life that, in Jacob, expressed God in His image and, in Joseph, represented God with His dominion (48:14-16; 41:40-44, 57):
Day 2   1. After Jacob was transformed and matured, he became the expression of God, becoming Israel, a corporate person (35:10).
   2. The exercise of God's dominion over all things was manifested in Joseph's life (45:8-9, 26a):
      a. Joseph's life under the heavenly vision was the life of the kingdom of the heavens described in Matthew 5—7.

b. Joseph's self-denial was the key to the practice of the kingdom life (Gen. 45:4-8; 50:15-21).

c. Because Joseph lived under God's restriction, the kingdom could be brought in through him (Matt. 16:24-28).

d. The reigning of Joseph in Egypt was the kingdom of God for the fulfillment of God's purpose (Gen. 41:55-57; 47:11-27; Rev. 11:15).

e. In Genesis 47 we have a picture of the millennium:

(1) Under Joseph, Egypt prefigured the millennium with all the people on the same level, without distinctions.

(2) Under Joseph's rule, the whole land of Egypt became a land of enjoyment:

(a) All the people were enjoyers on the same level because everyone and everything was under Joseph (vv. 14-21).

(b) This is a picture of the millennium, where everything will be under the Lord's hand (Psa. 24:1).

Day 3 II. **The matters of image and dominion, presented as seeds in Genesis, are developed and consummated in the New Testament:**

A. Christ's incarnation and God-man living fulfilled God's intention in His creation of man (Gen. 1:26-27; Luke 1:31-32, 35; 2:40, 52):

1. The incarnation of Christ and His God-man living are closely related to God's purpose that man would receive Him as life and express Him in His attributes (Gen. 1:26; 2:9; Acts 3:14a; Eph. 4:24).

2. When Christ came, He brought the kingdom of God with Him; the kingdom subdues rebellion, casts out demons, heals the sick,

and raises the dead (Luke 17:21; Matt. 12:28; Mark 4:35—5:43).

B. Whereas in Genesis 1 image precedes dominion, in the gospel the order is reversed, and dominion comes before image, because man has fallen from God's dominion and must repent (Mark 1:1, 14-15; Matt. 4:17):

1. Through the gospel of the kingdom, God brings rebellious people under the ruling of His authority so that they may become His kingdom and be ruled by His authority (24:14; Rev. 1:5-6):

   a. The gospel of the kingdom is proclaimed so that rebellious sinners might be saved, qualified, and equipped to enter into the kingdom of God (Acts 8:12).

   b. As believers in Christ, we have been regenerated to enter into the kingdom of God as the realm of the divine species to live under the rule of God in life (John 3:3, 5, 15-16).

Day 4   2. Christ is the image of God and the effulgence of His glory; hence, the gospel of Christ is the gospel of His glory that illuminates and shines forth (2 Cor. 4:3-4; Col. 1:15; Heb. 1:3):

   a. In 2 Corinthians 4:4 God is the image, the image is Christ, Christ is the glory, the glory is the gospel, and the gospel is the illumination.

   b. Through the illumination of the gospel of the glory of Christ, the shining reality of Christ, who is the embodiment and expression of the Triune God, is the treasure within us (vv. 6-7).

C. God intends that the believers in Christ be conformed to the image of the firstborn Son and that they reign in life (Rom. 8:29; 5:17):

1. Conformation to the image of God's Son issues

in His being the Firstborn among many brothers (8:29):

   a. Conformation denotes the shaping of life,
shaping us into the image of the firstborn
Son of God.

   b. Conformation is a process in which we are
saved in life from our self-likeness to be
conformed to the image of the firstborn
Son for His corporate expression (5:10).

2. God's complete salvation is for us to reign in
life by the abundance of grace and of the gift
of righteousness (vv. 17, 21):

   a. In experience, to reign in life is to be
under the ruling of the divine life, the
kingly and royal life with which we have
been regenerated (John 3:3, 5-6, 15-16;
Rom. 5:17).

   b. All the believers who have received the
abundance of grace and of the gift of
righteousness need to practice the restriction and limitation of the divine life
(Matt. 8:9; 2 Cor. 2:12-14; 5:14).

Day 5   D. As believers, we may know Christ as the image
of God and live in the kingdom of the Son of
God's love (Col. 1:15, 13):

1. God is invisible, but Christ as the Son of His
love, who is the effulgence of His glory and
the impress of His substance, is His image,
expressing what He is (Heb. 1:3; Col. 1:15).

2. To be transferred into the kingdom of the Son
of the Father's love is to be transferred into
the Son, the Beloved, who is life to us (v. 13;
1 John 5:11-12):

   a. Because the Father delights in His Son,
the kingdom of the Son is a pleasant thing,
a matter of delight (Matt. 3:17; 17:5).

   b. The kingdom in which we may live today
is a realm full of life, light, and love; in
this realm there is no fear (1 Pet. 2:9).

c. The church is the kingdom of the Son of the Father's love, which is as delightful to the Father as the Son is (Col. 1:13; 4:15-16).

E. The church as the one new man is the corporate man in God's intention; this universal new man will fulfill the twofold purpose of bearing God's image to express Him and exercising God's authority to represent Him and fight against God's enemy for God's kingdom (Eph. 2:15; 4:24; 6:10-20; Col. 3:10-11):

1. God's creation of man for His expression and representation is a picture, a type, of the universal new man in God's new creation (Gen. 1:26-28; Eph. 4:24).

2. The corporate new man bears the image of Him who created him (Col. 3:10), for the new man was "created according to God in righteousness and holiness of the reality" (Eph. 4:24).

Day 6

3. The one new man is a corporate warrior fighting against God's enemy to bring in God's kingdom (6:10-20; Rev. 12:10).

F. In the coming age, the age of the millennial kingdom, the glorious kingdom of God will be manifested on earth (Matt. 6:13; Rev. 11:15):

1. When the Lord Jesus comes again, He and the overcomers as the corporate smiting stone will become a great mountain to fill the whole earth, making the whole earth God's kingdom, His dominion (Dan. 2:34-35, 44-45).

2. The kingdom is a realm in which God exercises His power so that He can express His glory; thus, God's glory goes with His kingdom (Matt. 6:13; 1 Thes. 2:12).

3. In the millennium the overcoming believers will be with Christ in the bright glory of the kingdom, shining forth "like the sun in the kingdom of their Father" (Matt. 13:43).

G. The New Jerusalem in eternity is the consummation of image and dominion (Rev. 21:2, 10-11):

1. The New Jerusalem bears the image, the appearance, of God, expressing the Triune God
by her shining with a light "like a jasper
stone, as clear as crystal" (4:3; 21:10-11).

2. The New Jerusalem is the eternal kingdom
of God, filled with the glory of God (22:1, 5;
21:11).

Morning Nourishment

Gen. **And God said, Let Us make man in Our image,**
1:26 **according to Our likeness; and let them have do-**
minion...over all the earth and over every creeping
thing that creeps upon the earth.
28 **And God blessed them; and God said to them, Be**
fruitful and multiply, and fill the earth and subdue
it, and have dominion...

The record in the Bible has a purpose. Genesis, a book of
God's image and dominion, shows a complete picture of how
human beings can be remade and transformed to express God
in His image and to represent Him with His dominion. The last
fourteen chapters of Genesis indicate that after Jacob had
become Israel, he bore the image of God and exercised the dominion of God. The book of Genesis is complete; it ends the way
it begins. It begins and ends with God's image and dominion.
In the closing chapters of Genesis, God must have been happy,
and He could have said, "Now I have a man on earth expressing Me and representing Me. This man bears My image and
exercises My dominion. His words are My prophecy, and his
actions are the exercise of My dominion." This is the subject
of the book of Genesis. (*Life-study of Genesis*, pp. 1182-1183)

Today's Reading

Genesis 1:26 is a very crucial verse....Notice two significant
words here—*image* and *dominion*....We must consider in what
way and for what purpose man was created. The Bible says that
man was made in the image of God. Nothing is higher than God.
Thus, man was made in the image of the highest One. Perhaps
you have never regarded yourself this highly before. Because we
bear the divine image, we should have a high regard for ourselves.
We are not low creatures; we were made for the purpose of expressing God and exercising His dominion. The subject of Genesis is man bearing the image of God and exercising God's dominion over all things. We bear God's image that we might express
Him, and we have God's dominion that we might represent Him.

Man is God's Container ~ Open Vessel.

Therefore, we are God's expression and representation. This is the heart of Genesis. (*Life-study of Genesis*, p. 1180)

For God to create man in His image means that God created man with the intention that man would become a duplicate of God;...the word *image* implies that man has the capacity and ability to take God into him and to contain Him. The man created in God's image was created to be God's container....The word *likeness* refers to outward form, outward fashion, outward appearance. Hence, *likeness* here is a matter of expression. First, man was made in God's image to be a duplicate of God, and then man was made after God's likeness to have the appearance of God for His expression. (*Life-study of Luke*, p. 486)

God created a corporate man not only to express Himself with His image but also to represent Him by exercising His dominion over all things. God's intention in giving man dominion is (1) to subdue God's enemy, Satan, who rebelled against God; (2) to recover the earth, which was usurped by Satan; and (3) to exercise God's authority over the earth in order that the kingdom of God may come to the earth, the will of God may be done on the earth, and the glory of God may be manifested on the earth (Matt. 6:10, 13b). (Gen. 1:26, footnote 5)

We have seen that Jacob, God's expression, bore the image of God. But what about God's dominion? The book of Genesis ends with Joseph exercising dominion over the whole earth. Although Pharaoh was the king, he was merely a figurehead. The acting king was Joseph, who is a part of Jacob in the experience of life. In Jacob with Joseph we see the expression of God with the dominion of God. Never separate Joseph from Jacob. The record of the last fourteen chapters of Genesis mixes the two together. This indicates that Joseph is the reigning part of Jacob and that Jacob and Joseph should not be considered as separate persons. (*Life-study of Genesis*, p. 1182)

Further Reading: Life-study of Genesis, msg. 92; Life-study of Luke, msg. 56

Enlightenment and inspiration: _____

_____

_____

_____

Morning Nourishment

Gen. **And Joseph brought in Jacob his father and set**
47:7-8 **him before Pharaoh, and Jacob blessed Pharaoh.**
And Pharaoh said to Jacob, How many are the
years of your life?
Psa. **The earth is Jehovah's, and its fullness, the habit-**
24:1 **able land and those who dwell in it.**

[Jacob] was matured in life to become Israel. *El* in the name Israel means "God." God gave Jacob this name to signify that he had experienced God's dealing and had reached maturity. He was God's overcomer, God's prince. He was full of God's element and became God's expression.

Under God's sovereignty, through the sufferings in his circumstances and through God's direct dealing, Jacob was transformed and matured so that he became Israel. (*Truth Lessons—Level Two*, vol. 2, pp. 99-100)

Today's Reading

In the last few chapters of Genesis we see an Israel expressing God's image and exercising His dominion. The exercise of God's dominion over all things is manifested in Joseph's life, whereas God's image is expressed in Israel. Joseph is not separate from Jacob but is an aspect of the life that expresses God's image. The two aspects of expressing God's image and exercising God's dominion must be found in one person. Therefore, what is found in Joseph's life may be called the reigning aspect of the matured Israel. Without this light, you will not be able to understand this portion of the Word.

Joseph's life under the heavenly vision was the life of the kingdom of the heavens described in Matthew 5, 6, and 7. According to the constitution of the heavenly kingdom revealed in these chapters in Matthew, our anger must be subdued and our lust conquered (Matt. 5:21-32). If we claim to be the kingdom people, yet we cannot subdue our anger or conquer our lust, we are finished. Instead of being in the kingdom,…we are those giving vent to our anger and indulging in lust. But all the kingdom people subdue their anger and conquer their lust. This is the kingdom life.…We, the kingdom people in the kingdom life, are being trained to be kings, to be Josephs, to be the reigning aspect of the mature life.

Do you want to have a pleasant church life? Then you must be under restriction and deny yourself. We all need to learn this. Suppose Joseph had not been a self-denying person. In such a case it would have been impossible for the kingdom of God to be brought in and realized in a practical way. Joseph's self-denial, his restriction under God's sovereign hand, was the key to the practice of the kingdom life. Thank God for Joseph's self-denying life. Through such a life God's purpose was fulfilled, and the kingdom was brought in, realized, and practiced.

At the end of Genesis we find a seed of the truth of self-denial. In the closing chapters of Genesis, Christ is typified by Joseph, and the kingdom is foreshadowed by the house of Israel. Because Joseph denied himself, the kingdom of God could be realized in a practical way. The entire universe belongs to God, and God desires a kingdom. Although Pharaoh was ruling in Egypt, the kingdom of God was nonetheless realized through the reign of Joseph. The reigning of Joseph was the kingdom of God, which is for the fulfillment of God's purpose.

If you study Genesis 47, you will see that eventually the whole land of Egypt became a land of enjoyment. No longer were there distinctions between high and low and rich and poor. All the people became enjoyers on the same level because everyone and everything was under the same lord. This is a picture of the millennium. In the millennium there will be no capitalism or socialism. Everyone will be on the same level because everything will be under the Lord's hand. He will have bought everything, and He will have claimed everything and everyone. Truly the earth is the Lord's and the fullness thereof (Psa. 24:1)....Because Christ has claimed everything of us, we all are now on the same level enjoying the riches of Christ. (*Life-study of Genesis*, pp. 1409, 1428-1429, 1520, 1513, 1532)

Further Reading: Life-study of Genesis, msgs. 110-111, 119-120

Enlightenment and inspiration: _____

_____

_____

_____

Morning Nourishment

Matt. From that time Jesus began to proclaim and to say, Re-
4:17 pent, for the kingdom of the heavens has drawn near.
24:14 And this gospel of the kingdom will be preached in
     the whole inhabited earth for a testimony to all the
     nations, and then the end will come.

The two crucial words in chapter one of Genesis are *image*
and *dominion*. You may forget the creeping things and the fish,
but don't forget man with image and dominion. Man was not
made in the image of a serpent or scorpion but in the image
of God. This is the climax: man bearing God's image, exercising God's authority to maintain dominion.

Image and dominion were sown as two seeds in Genesis 1.
However, these seeds need the whole Bible to grow and develop.
The harvest, the full maturity, is in Revelation 21 and 22. (*Life-
study of Genesis,* p. 90)

Today's Reading

The Lord Jesus had a genuine man's living by God's mind,
will, and emotion—to express God in God's attributes. The
Lord did not seek His own will but God's will. He came not to
do His own will but to do God's will. This means that He came
to live as a man not by man's life, but by God's life. He lived by
God's mind, will, and emotion to express God in God's attributes. These attributes are contained in and mingled with His
human virtues. (*Life-study of Luke,* p. 524)

God is recovering His right over the earth in order to make
the whole earth His kingdom (Rev. 11:15). When Christ came, He
brought the kingdom of God with Him (Luke 17:21; Matt. 12:28).
This kingdom has been enlarged into the church (16:18-19),
which will accomplish the establishing of the kingdom of God on
the whole earth. (*The Conclusion of the New Testament,* p. 4127)

Human society, and every individual human being as well, is
full of "storms" of rebellion, demons, unclean industry (hog rais-
ing), death-sickness, and death. This is the actual situation of
mankind. But the Slave-Savior has brought the kingdom to us,

and the kingdom is the answer to the condition of fallen man. The kingdom subdues rebellion, the kingdom casts out demons, the kingdom clears up the unclean industry, the kingdom heals the sick, and the kingdom raises the dead. (*Life-study of Mark,* p. 162)

Some may ask why Genesis 1:26 and 28 mention expressing God with His image first and representing Him with His dominion second. The reason for this is that there we see God's original purpose. But because man has fallen, in the gospel man has to repent in order to come back to the beginning. Therefore, in the gospel, dominion is first and image follows. (*Life-study of Genesis,* p. 536)

On one hand, the Bible reveals the gospel as the gospel of grace, which is for us to become believers through faith. On the other hand, the Bible says that the gospel is the gospel of the kingdom, which is for us to become the Lord's disciples, those who are trained, ruled, disciplined, and dealt with by the Lord's authority. According to the gospel of grace, God is pleased to freely grant us grace, and we can receive this grace simply by believing. However, this gospel is also the gospel of the kingdom through which God desires to bring us under the ruling of the heavenly authority so that we may become His kingdom, those who are ruled by God's authority. (*What the Kingdom Is to the Believers,* p. 88)

Satan instigated man to rebel against God by building the city and tower of Babel. The building of the city and tower of Babel was a declaration of independence from God. Mankind was declaring that it had become independent of God.

The gospel is for the kingdom. The purpose of the preaching of the gospel is that men might enter into the kingdom. The gospel is proclaimed that people might be saved, qualified, and equipped to enter into the kingdom....The gospel of the kingdom brings the rebellious sinners into the church. But now we need to see what is the reality of the church. The reality of the church is the kingdom. (*Life-study of Genesis,* pp. 470-471)

Further Reading: Life-study of Genesis, msg. 35; *Life-study of Mark,* msg. 13

Enlightenment and inspiration: _____

_____

_____

_____

Morning Nourishment

Rom. Because those whom He foreknew, He also predes-
8:29 tinated *to be* conformed to the image of His Son, that
He might be the Firstborn among many brothers.

5:17 For if, by the offense of the one, death reigned
through the one, much more those who receive the
abundance of grace and of the gift of righteousness
will reign in life through the One, Jesus Christ.

In 2 Corinthians 4:4 Paul says that "the illumination of the
gospel of the glory of Christ, who is the image of God, might
not shine on them." This verse indicates that the terms *God,
image, Christ, glory, gospel,* and *illumination* are all in appo-
sition to one another; thus, they all refer to the same wonderful person. God is the image, the image is Christ, Christ is the
glory, the glory is the gospel, and the gospel is the illumination.
(*The Conclusion of the New Testament,* p. 3206)

Today's Reading

We reign in life in being conformed to the image of God's
firstborn Son through the Spirit's interceding that all things
may work together for the conformation of those who love God
(Rom. 8:26-29). (*Crystallization-study of the Complete Salvation of God in Romans,* p. 30)

Conformation is the end result of transformation. It includes
the changing of our inward essence and nature, and it also includes the changing of our outward form, that we may match
the glorified image of Christ, the God-man. He is the prototype
and we are the mass production. (Rom. 8:29, footnote 3)

Christ was the only begotten Son of God from eternity (John
1:18). When He was sent by God into the world, He was still
the only begotten Son of God (1 John 4:9; John 1:14; 3:16). By
His passing through death and entering into resurrection, His
humanity was uplifted into His divinity. Thus, in His divinity
with His humanity that passed through death and resurrection, He was born in resurrection as God's firstborn Son
(Acts 13:33). At the same time, all His believers were raised

together with Him in His resurrection (1 Pet. 1:3) and were begotten together with Him as the many sons of God. Thus they became His many brothers to constitute His Body and be God's corporate expression in Him. (Rom. 8:29, footnote 4)

Conformation denotes the shaping of life. As the divine life grows within us and transforms us, it spontaneously shapes us into the pattern, the image, of the firstborn Son of God. Self-likeness is the expression, the appearance, of the self...We need to be saved in the life of Christ from such a self-expression.... To be saved from the self is to be conformed to the image of the Son of God. This means that to be saved from the self is to be made truly a son of God. (*Life-study of Romans,* pp. 683, 492)

God's complete salvation is for us to reign in life by the abundance of grace (God Himself as our all-sufficient supply for our organic salvation) and of the gift of righteousness (God's judicial redemption applied to us in a practical way). When we are all reigning in life, living under the ruling of the divine life, the issue is the real and practical Body life. (*Crystallization-study of the Complete Salvation of God in Romans,* p. 37)

To be saved in life causes us to reign as kings [Rom. 5:17]....A justified person should reign because he has the divine life, a kingly life, with which to reign. Without the kingly life, no one can reign. When we were redeemed by Christ, forgiven of our sins, and washed by the blood of Christ, we were justified. In addition, we were regenerated with a divine, spiritual, heavenly, kingly, and royal life. Thus, we are now able to reign in life as kings. (*To Be Saved in the Life of Christ as Revealed in Romans,* pp. 9-10)

Today there is the need for all the believers who have received the abundance of grace and of the gift of righteousness to practice the life restriction and limitation in the divine life. (*Crystallization-study of the Complete Salvation of God in Romans,* p. 43)

Further Reading: Life-study of 2 Corinthians, msg. 9; *Crystallization-study of the Complete Salvation of God in Romans,* msg. 4; *Salvation in Life in the Book of Romans,* ch. 7

Enlightenment and inspiration: _____

_____
_____
_____

Morning Nourishment

Col. Who delivered us out of the authority of darkness and
1:13 transferred *us* into the kingdom of the Son of His love.
Eph. And put on the new man, which was created accord-
4:24 ing to God in righteousness and holiness of the reality.

For Christ to be the Head of the Body, and for us, His believers, to be the members of His Body, God needed to deliver us
out of the authority of darkness, the kingdom of Satan (Matt.
12:26b), and transfer us into the kingdom of the Son of His love.
This is to qualify us to partake of the all-inclusive Christ as
our allotted portion. (Col. 1:13, footnote 1)

God is invisible. But the Son of His love, who is the effulgence of His glory and the impress of His substance (Heb. 1:3),
is His image, expressing what He is. The image here is not a
physical form but an expression of God's being in all His attributes and virtues (Col. 1:15, footnote 1)

Today's Reading

To be transferred into the kingdom of the Son of the Father's
love is to be transferred into the Son who is life to us (1 John
5:12). The Son in resurrection (1 Pet. 1:3; Rom. 6:4-5) is now the
life-giving Spirit (1 Cor. 15:45b). He rules us in His resurrection
life with love. This is the kingdom of the Son of the Father's
love. When we live by the Son as our life in resurrection, we
are living in His kingdom, enjoying Him in the Father's love.
(*Life-study of Colossians,* pp. 34-35)

According to the New Testament, the Son of God is the
expression of the divine life and its embodiment. This means
that the kingdom of the Son is a realm of life. The fact that the
kingdom into which we have been transferred is the kingdom
of the Son of God's love indicates that this realm of life is in
love, not in fear. The kingdom in which we find ourselves today
is a realm full of life, light, and love.

The words *the Son of God* are a delight to the Father's ears. When
the Lord Jesus was baptized, the Father declared, "This is My Son,
the Beloved, in whom I have found My delight" (Matt. 3:17). When

the Lord was transfigured, the Father made the same declaration
(Matt. 17:5). Because the Father delights in His Son, the kingdom of
the Son of the Father's love is a pleasant thing, a matter of delight.

The stress in Colossians 1:13 is the kingdom of the Son of
God's love in this age, which is the reality of the church. The
church life today is the kingdom of the Son of God's love, which
is as delightful to God the Father as the Son of God is. We, the
believers, all have been transferred into this delightful kingdom
of the Son of God's love. God the Father loves the delightful part
of the kingdom, just as He loves His delightful Son as His own.

God's creation of man in Genesis 1 is a picture of the new man
in God's new creation. This means that the old creation is a figure,
a type, of the new creation. In God's old creation the central character is man. It is the same in God's new creation. Therefore, in
both the old creation and the new creation man is the center.

Eventually, the church as the new man is the man in God's
intention. God wanted a man, and in the old creation He created a figure, a type, not the real man. The real man is the man
Christ created on the cross through His all-inclusive death.
This man is called the new man.

The old man did not fulfill God's dual purpose. However, the
new man in God's new creation does fulfill the twofold purpose
of expressing God and dealing with God's enemy. (*The Conclusion of the New Testament,* pp. 2582-2584, 2302-2303)

The old man was created outwardly according to the image of
God but without God's life and nature (Gen. 1:26-27), whereas
the new man was created inwardly according to God Himself and
with God's life and nature (Col. 3:10). (Eph. 4:24, footnote 3)

In the life of Jesus, righteousness and holiness of the reality
were continuously manifested. It was in the righteousness and
holiness of this reality, which is God realized and expressed,
that the new man was created. (Eph. 4:24, footnote 5)

Further Reading: Life-study of Colossians, msgs. 4, 10, 28, 62;
The Conclusion of the New Testament, msgs. 216, 352

Enlightenment and inspiration: _____

_____

_____

_____

Morning Nourishment

Matt. ...For Yours is the kingdom and the power and the
6:13 glory forever. Amen.
Rev. Having the glory of God. Her light was like a most
21:11 precious stone, like a jasper stone, as clear as crystal.

There are many believers, but there is only one new man in
the universe. All the believers are components of this corporate
and universal new man. According to Ephesians 4:13, we are to
grow up until we arrive at a full-grown man, and in 4:24 we see
that, in a practical way, we need to put on the new man.

In chapter 6 we see that the church is a warrior to defeat
God's enemy, the devil. In order to fight the spiritual warfare, we
need both the power of the Lord and also the whole armor of
God. The church is a corporate warrior, and the believers are parts
of this unique warrior. We must fight the spiritual warfare in the
Body, not individually. (*Life-study of Ephesians,* pp. 622-623)

Today's Reading

According to Daniel 2:35 and 44, Christ will come as the stone
cut out without hands to crush the great human image from the
toes to the head....However, He will not come by Himself; He
will come with His bride (Rev. 19:11, 14). Before His coming He
will have a wedding, uniting His overcomers to Himself as one
entity (vv. 7-9). Whereas Daniel 2 speaks of Christ coming as a
stone cut out without hands, Revelation 19 speaks of Christ coming as the One who has His bride as His army....After crushing
the human government, God will have cleared up the entire universe. The old creation will be gone, and the human government
will become chaff blown away by the wind. Then the corporate
Christ, Christ with His overcomers, will become a great mountain to fill the whole earth, making the whole earth God's kingdom (Dan. 2:35, 44). Both the earth and the heaven will then be
new for God to exercise His kingdom. (*Life-study of Daniel,* p. 75)

In the coming age, the entering into the kingdom of God and
the entering into the glory of God will take place simultaneously.
When we live by the divine life, the life of God, we surely will

express God, and the expressed God is the divine glory. Since we live such a life, we are in the divine glory. Then spontaneously we are in the kingdom of God, because the kingdom of God is just God's manifestation in His glory with His authority for His divine administration. Hence, to enter into the kingdom of God and to enter into the expressed glory of God transpire at the same time as one thing.... [Matthew 6:13] indicates that God's glory goes with His kingdom and is expressed in the realm of His kingdom. The kingdom is the realm for God to exercise His power that He may express His glory. (*The Conclusion of the New Testament*, p. 2662)

At the Lord's coming, He will take away only the overcomers, leaving the rest of the believers in another category because they will not have the maturity in His divine life. In the millennium the overcoming believers will be with Christ in the bright glory of the kingdom. (*The Overcomers*, p. 10)

The whole New Jerusalem expresses God, bearing God's appearance. The New Jerusalem also exercises God's divine authority to maintain God's dominion for eternity. Today, these two seeds are growing in you and me. The image of God and the authority of God are constantly growing within us. (*Life-study of Genesis*, p. 90)

Jasper is the appearance of God (Rev. 4:3). Hence, the jasper wall [in 21:11] signifies that the whole city, as the corporate expression of God in eternity, bears the appearance of God. When we are in New Jerusalem, we shall marvel to see that the whole city has the same appearance, the appearance of jasper. (*Life-study of Revelation*, p. 699)

The nations will walk by the light of the New Jerusalem, an organic building. Thus, the entire eternal kingdom of God will be under the shining of God's glory in the Redeemer through the redeemed as the diffuser. The eternal kingdom of God includes the New Jerusalem and the nations around it. (*The Conclusion of the New Testament*, p. 4461)

Further Reading: The Conclusion of the New Testament, msgs. 245, 247-249

Enlightenment and inspiration: _____

_____

_____

_____

Hymns, #941

1 God's kingdom is God's reigning,
     His glory to maintain;
It is His sovereign ruling,
     His order to sustain.
He exercises fully
     His own authority
Within His kingdom ever
     And to eternity.

2 Upon the throne, the center
     Of government divine,
God reigns, and with His purpose
     Brings everything in line.
God's headship and His lordship
     He only can maintain
As King within His kingdom,
     O'er everything to reign.

3 By reigning in His kingdom
     God worketh all His will,
And under His dominion
     His purpose doth fulfill.
'Tis only in God's kingdom
     His blessing we may know;
'Tis from His throne almighty
     The stream of life doth flow.

4 Submitted to God's ruling,
     All virtue thus will win;
Rebellion to His Headship
     Is but the root of sin.
The evil aim of Satan —
     God's throne to overthrow;
Our aim and goal is ever
     His rule to fully know.

5 Within God's sovereign kingdom
     His Christ is magnified;
When Christ in life is reigning,
     The Father's glorified.
When God is in dominion,
     All things are truly blessed;
When Christ for God is reigning,
     God's glory is expressed.

6   In fulness of the seasons
      God's Christ will head up all,
   Then all will own His reigning
      And worship, great and small.
   Such reign in life and glory
      The Church e'en now foretastes,
   And to His rule submitting
      Unto His kingdom hastes.

Composition for prophecy with main point and sub-points: _____

_____
_____
_____
_____
_____
_____
_____
_____
_____
_____
_____
_____
_____
_____
_____
_____
_____
_____
_____
_____
_____
_____
_____
_____
_____
_____
_____

Reading Schedule for the Recovery Version of the Old Testament with Footnotes

Wk.	Lord's Day	Monday	Tuesday	Wednesday	Thursday	Friday	Saturday
1	Gen. 1:1-5 ☐	1:6-23 ☐	1:24-31 ☐	2:1-9 ☐	2:10-25 ☐	3:1-13 ☐	3:14-24 ☐
2	4:1-26 ☐	5:1-32 ☐	6:1-22 ☐	7:1—8:3 ☐	8:4-22 ☐	9:1-29 ☐	10:1-32 ☐
3	11:1-32 ☐	12:1-20 ☐	13:1-18 ☐	14:1-24 ☐	15:1-21 ☐	16:1-16 ☐	17:1-27 ☐
4	18:1-33 ☐	19:1-38 ☐	20:1-18 ☐	21:1-34 ☐	22:1-24 ☐	23:1—24:27 ☐	24:28-67 ☐
5	25:1-34 ☐	26:1-35 ☐	27:1-46 ☐	28:1-22 ☐	29:1-35 ☐	30:1-43 ☐	31:1-55 ☐
6	32:1-32 ☐	33:1—34:31 ☐	35:1-29 ☐	36:1-43 ☐	37:1-36 ☐	38:1—39:23 ☐	40:1—41:13 ☐
7	41:14-57 ☐	42:1-38 ☐	43:1-34 ☐	44:1-34 ☐	45:1-28 ☐	46:1-34 ☐	47:1-31 ☐
8	48:1-22 ☐	49:1-15 ☐	49:16-33 ☐	50:1-26 ☐	Exo. 1:1-22 ☐	2:1-25 ☐	3:1-22 ☐
9	4:1-31 ☐	5:1-23 ☐	6:1-30 ☐	7:1-25 ☐	8:1-32 ☐	9:1-35 ☐	10:1-29 ☐
10	11:1-10 ☐	12:1-14 ☐	12:15-36 ☐	12:37-51 ☐	13:1-22 ☐	14:1-31 ☐	15:1-27 ☐
11	16:1-36 ☐	17:1-16 ☐	18:1-27 ☐	19:1-25 ☐	20:1-26 ☐	21:1-36 ☐	22:1-31 ☐
12	23:1-33 ☐	24:1-18 ☐	25:1-22 ☐	25:23-40 ☐	26:1-14 ☐	26:15-37 ☐	27:1-21 ☐
13	28:1-21 ☐	28:22-43 ☐	29:1-21 ☐	29:22-46 ☐	30:1-10 ☐	30:11-38 ☐	31:1-17 ☐
14	31:18—32:35 ☐	33:1-23 ☐	34:1-35 ☐	35:1-35 ☐	36:1-38 ☐	37:1-29 ☐	38:1-31 ☐
15	39:1-43 ☐	40:1-38 ☐	Lev. 1:1-17 ☐	2:1-16 ☐	3:1-17 ☐	4:1-35 ☐	5:1-19 ☐
16	6:1-30 ☐	7:1-38 ☐	8:1-36 ☐	9:1-24 ☐	10:1-20 ☐	11:1-47 ☐	12:1-8 ☐
17	13:1-28 ☐	13:29-59 ☐	14:1-18 ☐	14:19-32 ☐	14:33-57 ☐	15:1-33 ☐	16:1-17 ☐
18	16:18-34 ☐	17:1-16 ☐	18:1-30 ☐	19:1-37 ☐	20:1-27 ☐	21:1-24 ☐	22:1-33 ☐
19	23:1-22 ☐	23:23-44 ☐	24:1-23 ☐	25:1-23 ☐	25:24-55 ☐	26:1-24 ☐	26:25-46 ☐
20	27:1-34 ☐	Num. 1:1-54 ☐	2:1-34 ☐	3:1-51 ☐	4:1-49 ☐	5:1-31 ☐	6:1-27 ☐
21	7:1-41 ☐	7:42-88 ☐	7:89—8:26 ☐	9:1-23 ☐	10:1-36 ☐	11:1-35 ☐	12:1—13:33 ☐
22	14:1-45 ☐	15:1-41 ☐	16:1-50 ☐	17:1—18:7 ☐	18:8-32 ☐	19:1-22 ☐	20:1-29 ☐
23	21:1-35 ☐	22:1-41 ☐	23:1-30 ☐	24:1-25 ☐	25:1-18 ☐	26:1-65 ☐	27:1-23 ☐
24	28:1-31 ☐	29:1-40 ☐	30:1—31:24 ☐	31:25-54 ☐	32:1-42 ☐	33:1-56 ☐	34:1-29 ☐
25	35:1-34 ☐	36:1-13 ☐	Deut. 1:1-46 ☐	2:1-37 ☐	3:1-29 ☐	4:1-49 ☐	5:1-33 ☐
26	6:1—7:26 ☐	8:1-20 ☐	9:1-29 ☐	10:1-22 ☐	11:1-32 ☐	12:1-32 ☐	13:1—14:21 ☐

Reading Schedule for the Recovery Version of the Old Testament with Footnotes

Wk.	Lord's Day	Monday	Tuesday	Wednesday	Thursday	Friday	Saturday
27	14:22—15:23 ☐	16:1-22 ☐	17:1—18:8 ☐	18:9—19:21 ☐	20:1—21:17 ☐	21:18—22:30 ☐	23:1-25 ☐
28	24:1-22 ☐	25:1-19 ☐	26:1-19 ☐	27:1-26 ☐	28:1-68 ☐	29:1-29 ☐	30:1—31:29 ☐
29	31:30—32:52 ☐	33:1-29 ☐	34:1-12 ☐	Josh. 1:1-18 ☐	2:1-24 ☐	3:1-17 ☐	4:1-24 ☐
30	5:1-15 ☐	6:1-27 ☐	7:1-26 ☐	8:1-35 ☐	9:1-27 ☐	10:1-43 ☐	11:1—12:24 ☐
31	13:1-33 ☐	14:1—15:63 ☐	16:1—18:28 ☐	19:1-51 ☐	20:1—21:45 ☐	22:1-34 ☐	23:1—24:33 ☐
32	Judg. 1:1-36 ☐	2:1-23 ☐	3:1-31 ☐	4:1-24 ☐	5:1-31 ☐	6:1-40 ☐	7:1-25 ☐
33	8:1-35 ☐	9:1-57 ☐	10:1—11:40 ☐	12:1—13:25 ☐	14:1—15:20 ☐	16:1-31 ☐	17:1—18:31 ☐
34	19:1-30 ☐	20:1-48 ☐	21:1-25 ☐	Ruth 1:1-22 ☐	2:1-23 ☐	3:1-18 ☐	4:1-22 ☐
35	1 Sam. 1:1-28 ☐	2:1-36 ☐	3:1—4:22 ☐	5:1—6:21 ☐	7:1—8:22 ☐	9:1-27 ☐	10:1—11:15 ☐
36	12:1—13:23 ☐	14:1-52 ☐	15:1-35 ☐	16:1-23 ☐	17:1-58 ☐	18:1-30 ☐	19:1-24 ☐
37	20:1-42 ☐	21:1—22:23 ☐	23:1—24:22 ☐	25:1-44 ☐	26:1-25 ☐	27:1—28:25 ☐	29:1—30:31 ☐
38	31:1-13 ☐	2 Sam. 1:1-27 ☐	2:1-32 ☐	3:1-39 ☐	4:1—5:25 ☐	6:1-23 ☐	7:1-29 ☐
39	8:1—9:13 ☐	10:1—11:27 ☐	12:1-31 ☐	13:1-39 ☐	14:1-33 ☐	15:1—16:23 ☐	17:1—18:33 ☐
40	19:1-43 ☐	20:1—21:22 ☐	22:1-51 ☐	23:1-39 ☐	24:1-25 ☐	1 Kings 1:1-19 ☐	1:20-53 ☐
41	2:1-46 ☐	3:1-28 ☐	4:1-34 ☐	5:1—6:38 ☐	7:1-22 ☐	7:23-51 ☐	8:1-36 ☐
42	8:37-66 ☐	9:1-28 ☐	10:1-29 ☐	11:1-43 ☐	12:1-33 ☐	13:1-34 ☐	14:1-31 ☐
43	15:1-34 ☐	16:1—17:24 ☐	18:1-46 ☐	19:1-21 ☐	20:1-43 ☐	21:1—22:53 ☐	2 Kings 1:1-18 ☐
44	2:1—3:27 ☐	4:1-44 ☐	5:1—6:33 ☐	7:1-20 ☐	8:1-29 ☐	9:1-37 ☐	10:1-36 ☐
45	11:1—12:21 ☐	13:1—14:29 ☐	15:1-38 ☐	16:1-20 ☐	17:1-41 ☐	18:1-37 ☐	19:1-37 ☐
46	20:1—21:26 ☐	22:1-20 ☐	23:1-37 ☐	24:1—25:30 ☐	1 Chron. 1:1-54 ☐	2:1—3:24 ☐	4:1—5:26 ☐
47	6:1-81 ☐	7:1-40 ☐	8:1-40 ☐	9:1-44 ☐	10:1—11:47 ☐	12:1-40 ☐	13:1—14:17 ☐
48	15:1—16:43 ☐	17:1-27 ☐	18:1—19:19 ☐	20:1—21:30 ☐	22:1—23:32 ☐	24:1—25:31 ☐	26:1-32 ☐
49	27:1-34 ☐	28:1—29:30 ☐	2 Chron. 1:1-17 ☐	2:1—3:17 ☐	4:1—5:14 ☐	6:1-42 ☐	7:1—8:18 ☐
50	9:1—10:19 ☐	11:1—12:16 ☐	13:1—15:19 ☐	16:1—17:19 ☐	18:1—19:11 ☐	20:1-37 ☐	21:1—22:12 ☐
51	23:1—24:27 ☐	25:1—26:23 ☐	27:1—28:27 ☐	29:1-36 ☐	30:1—31:21 ☐	32:1-33 ☐	33:1—34:33 ☐
52	35:1—36:23 ☐	Ezra 1:1-11 ☐	2:1-70 ☐	3:1—4:24 ☐	5:1—6:22 ☐	7:1-28 ☐	8:1-36 ☐

Reading Schedule for the Recovery Version of the Old Testament with Footnotes

Wk.	Lord's Day	Monday	Tuesday	Wednesday	Thursday	Friday	Saturday
53	9:1—10:44 ☐	Neh. 1:1-11 ☐	2:1—3:32 ☐	4:1—5:19 ☐	6:1-19 ☐	7:1-73 ☐	8:1-18 ☐
54	9:1-20 ☐	9:21-38 ☐	10:1—11:36 ☐	12:1-47 ☐	13:1-31 ☐	Esth. 1:1-22 ☐	2:1—3:15 ☐
55	4:1—5:14 ☐	6:1—7:10 ☐	8:1-17 ☐	9:1—10:3 ☐	Job 1:1-22 ☐	2:1—3:26 ☐	4:1—5:27 ☐
56	6:1—7:21 ☐	8:1—9:35 ☐	10:1—11:20 ☐	12:1—13:28 ☐	14:1—15:35 ☐	16:1—17:16 ☐	18:1—19:29 ☐
57	20:1—21:34 ☐	22:1—23:17 ☐	24:1—25:6 ☐	26:1—27:23 ☐	28:1—29:25 ☐	30:1—31:40 ☐	32:1—33:33 ☐
58	34:1—35:16 ☐	36:1-33 ☐	37:1-24 ☐	38:1-41 ☐	39:1-30 ☐	40:1-24 ☐	41:1-34 ☐
59	42:1-17 ☐	Psa. 1:1-6 ☐	2:1—3:8 ☐	4:1—6:10 ☐	7:1—8:9 ☐	9:1—10:18 ☐	11:1—15:5 ☐
60	16:1—17:15 ☐	18:1-50 ☐	19:1—21:13 ☐	22:1-31 ☐	23:1—24:10 ☐	25:1—27:14 ☐	28:1—30:12 ☐
61	31:1—32:11 ☐	33:1—34:22 ☐	35:1—36:12 ☐	37:1-40 ☐	38:1—39:13 ☐	40:1—41:13 ☐	42:1—43:5 ☐
62	44:1-26 ☐	45:1-17 ☐	46:1—48:14 ☐	49:1—50:23 ☐	51:1—52:9 ☐	53:1—55:23 ☐	56:1—58:11 ☐
63	59:1—61:8 ☐	62:1—64:10 ☐	65:1—67:7 ☐	68:1-35 ☐	69:1—70:5 ☐	71:1—72:20 ☐	73:1—74:23 ☐
64	75:1—77:20 ☐	78:1-72 ☐	79:1—81:16 ☐	82:1—84:12 ☐	85:1—87:7 ☐	88:1—89:52 ☐	90:1—91:16 ☐
65	92:1—94:23 ☐	95:1—97:12 ☐	98:1—101:8 ☐	102:1—103:22 ☐	104:1—105:45 ☐	106:1-48 ☐	107:1-43 ☐
66	108:1—109:31 ☐	110:1—112:10 ☐	113:1—115:18 ☐	116:1—118:29 ☐	119:1-32 ☐	119:33-72 ☐	119:73-120 ☐
67	119:121-176 ☐	120:1—124:8 ☐	125:1—128:6 ☐	129:1—132:18 ☐	133:1—135:21 ☐	136:1—138:8 ☐	139:1—140:13 ☐
68	141:1—144:15 ☐	145:1—147:20 ☐	148:1—150:6 ☐	Prov. 1:1-33 ☐	2:1—3:35 ☐	4:1—5:23 ☐	6:1-35 ☐
69	7:1—8:36 ☐	9:1—10:32 ☐	11:1—12:28 ☐	13:1—14:35 ☐	15:1-33 ☐	16:1-33 ☐	17:1-28 ☐
70	18:1-24 ☐	19:1—20:30 ☐	21:1—22:29 ☐	23:1-35 ☐	24:1—25:28 ☐	26:1—27:27 ☐	28:1—29:27 ☐
71	30:1-33 ☐	31:1-31 ☐	Eccl. 1:1-18 ☐	2:1—3:22 ☐	4:1—5:20 ☐	6:1—7:29 ☐	8:1—9:18 ☐
72	10:1—11:10 ☐	12:1-14 ☐	S.S. 1:1-8 ☐	1:9-17 ☐	2:1-17 ☐	3:1-11 ☐	4:1-8 ☐
73	4:9-16 ☐	5:1-16 ☐	6:1-13 ☐	7:1-13 ☐	8:1-14 ☐	Isa. 1:1-11 ☐	1:12-31 ☐
74	2:1-22 ☐	3:1-26 ☐	4:1-6 ☐	5:1-30 ☐	6:1-13 ☐	7:1-25 ☐	8:1-22 ☐
75	9:1-21 ☐	10:1-34 ☐	11:1—12:6 ☐	13:1-22 ☐	14:1-14 ☐	14:15-32 ☐	15:1—16:14 ☐
76	17:1—18:7 ☐	19:1-25 ☐	20:1—21:17 ☐	22:1-25 ☐	23:1-18 ☐	24:1-23 ☐	25:1-12 ☐
77	26:1-21 ☐	27:1-13 ☐	28:1-29 ☐	29:1-24 ☐	30:1-33 ☐	31:1—32:20 ☐	33:1-24 ☐
78	34:1-17 ☐	35:1-10 ☐	36:1-22 ☐	37:1-38 ☐	38:1—39:8 ☐	40:1-31 ☐	41:1-29 ☐

Reading Schedule for the Recovery Version of the Old Testament with Footnotes

Wk.	Lord's Day	Monday	Tuesday	Wednesday	Thursday	Friday	Saturday
79	42:1-25 ☐	43:1-28 ☐	44:1-28 ☐	45:1-25 ☐	46:1-13 ☐	47:1-15 ☐	48:1-22 ☐
80	49:1-13 ☐	49:14-26 ☐	50:1—51:23 ☐	52:1-15 ☐	53:1-12 ☐	54:1-17 ☐	55:1-13 ☐
81	56:1-12 ☐	57:1-21 ☐	58:1-14 ☐	59:1-21 ☐	60:1-22 ☐	61:1-11 ☐	62:1-12 ☐
82	63:1-19 ☐	64:1-12 ☐	65:1-25 ☐	66:1-24 ☐	Jer. 1:1-19 ☐	2:1-19 ☐	2:20-37 ☐
83	3:1-25 ☐	4:1-31 ☐	5:1-31 ☐	6:1-30 ☐	7:1-34 ☐	8:1-22 ☐	9:1-26 ☐
84	10:1-25 ☐	11:1—12:17 ☐	13:1-27 ☐	14:1-22 ☐	15:1-21 ☐	16:1—17:27 ☐	18:1-23 ☐
85	19:1—20:18 ☐	21:1—22:30 ☐	23:1-40 ☐	24:1—25:38 ☐	26:1—27:22 ☐	28:1—29:32 ☐	30:1-24 ☐
86	31:1-23 ☐	31:24-40 ☐	32:1-44 ☐	33:1-26 ☐	34:1-22 ☐	35:1-19 ☐	36:1-32 ☐
87	37:1-21 ☐	38:1-28 ☐	39:1—40:16 ☐	41:1—42:22 ☐	43:1—44:30 ☐	45:1—46:28 ☐	47:1—48:16 ☐
88	48:17-47 ☐	49:1-22 ☐	49:23-39 ☐	50:1-27 ☐	50:28-46 ☐	51:1-27 ☐	51:28-64 ☐
89	52:1-34 ☐	Lam. 1:1-22 ☐	2:1-22 ☐	3:1-39 ☐	3:40-66 ☐	4:1-22 ☐	5:1-22 ☐
90	Ezek. 1:1-14 ☐	1:15-28 ☐	2:1—3:27 ☐	4:1—5:17 ☐	6:1—7:27 ☐	8:1—9:11 ☐	10:1—11:25 ☐
91	12:1—13:23 ☐	14:1—15:8 ☐	16:1-63 ☐	17:1—18:32 ☐	19:1-14 ☐	20:1-49 ☐	21:1-32 ☐
92	22:1-31 ☐	23:1-49 ☐	24:1-27 ☐	25:1—26:21 ☐	27:1-36 ☐	28:1-26 ☐	29:1—30:26 ☐
93	31:1—32:32 ☐	33:1-33 ☐	34:1-31 ☐	35:1—36:21 ☐	36:22-38 ☐	37:1-28 ☐	38:1—39:29 ☐
94	40:1-27 ☐	40:28-49 ☐	41:1-26 ☐	42:1—43:27 ☐	44:1-31 ☐	45:1-25 ☐	46:1-24 ☐
95	47:1-23 ☐	48:1-35 ☐	Dan. 1:1-21 ☐	2:1-30 ☐	2:31-49 ☐	3:1-30 ☐	4:1-37 ☐
96	5:1-31 ☐	6:1-28 ☐	7:1-12 ☐	7:13-28 ☐	8:1-27 ☐	9:1-27 ☐	10:1-21 ☐
97	11:1-22 ☐	11:23-45 ☐	12:1-13 ☐	Hosea 1:1-11 ☐	2:1-23 ☐	3:1—4:19 ☐	5:1-15 ☐
98	6:1-11 ☐	7:1-16 ☐	8:1-14 ☐	9:1-17 ☐	10:1-15 ☐	11:1-12 ☐	12:1-14 ☐
99	13:1—14:9 ☐	Joel 1:1-20 ☐	2:1-16 ☐	2:17-32 ☐	3:1-21 ☐	Amos 1:1-15 ☐	2:1-16 ☐
100	3:1-15 ☐	4:1—5:27 ☐	6:1—7:17 ☐	8:1—9:15 ☐	Obad. 1-21 ☐	Jonah 1:1-17 ☐	2:1—4:11 ☐
101	Micah 1:1-16 ☐	2:1—3:12 ☐	4:1—5:15 ☐	6:1—7:20 ☐	Nahum 1:1-15 ☐	2:1—3:19 ☐	Hab. 1:1-17 ☐
102	2:1-20 ☐	3:1-19 ☐	Zeph. 1:1-18 ☐	2:1-15 ☐	3:1-20 ☐	Hag. 1:1-15 ☐	2:1-23 ☐
103	Zech. 1:1-21 ☐	2:1-13 ☐	3:1-10 ☐	4:1-14 ☐	5:1—6:15 ☐	7:1—8:23 ☐	9:1-17 ☐
104	10:1—11:17 ☐	12:1—13:9 ☐	14:1-21 ☐	Mal. 1:1-14 ☐	2:1-17 ☐	3:1-18 ☐	4:1-6 ☐

Reading Schedule for the Recovery Version of the New Testament with Footnotes

Wk.	Lord's Day	Monday	Tuesday	Wednesday	Thursday	Friday	Saturday
1	Matt. 1:1-2 ☐	1:3-7 ☐	1:8-17 ☐	1:18-25 ☐	2:1-23 ☐	3:1-6 ☐	3:7-17 ☐
2	4:1-11 ☐	4:12-25 ☐	5:1-4 ☐	5:5-12 ☐	5:13-20 ☐	5:21-26 ☐	5:27-48 ☐
3	6:1-8 ☐	6:9-18 ☐	6:19-34 ☐	7:1-12 ☐	7:13-29 ☐	8:1-13 ☐	8:14-22 ☐
4	8:23-34 ☐	9:1-13 ☐	9:14-17 ☐	9:18-34 ☐	9:35—10:5 ☐	10:6-25 ☐	10:26-42 ☐
5	11:1-15 ☐	11:16-30 ☐	12:1-14 ☐	12:15-32 ☐	12:33-42 ☐	12:43—13:2 ☐	13:3-12 ☐
6	13:13-30 ☐	13:31-43 ☐	13:44-58 ☐	14:1-13 ☐	14:14-21 ☐	14:22-36 ☐	15:1-20 ☐
7	15:21-31 ☐	15:32-39 ☐	16:1-12 ☐	16:13-20 ☐	16:21-28 ☐	17:1-13 ☐	17:14-27 ☐
8	18:1-14 ☐	18:15-22 ☐	18:23-35 ☐	19:1-15 ☐	19:16-30 ☐	20:1-16 ☐	20:17-34 ☐
9	21:1-11 ☐	21:12-22 ☐	21:23-32 ☐	21:33-46 ☐	22:1-22 ☐	22:23-33 ☐	22:34-46 ☐
10	23:1-12 ☐	23:13-39 ☐	24:1-14 ☐	24:15-31 ☐	24:32-51 ☐	25:1-13 ☐	25:14-30 ☐
11	25:31-46 ☐	26:1-16 ☐	26:17-35 ☐	26:36-46 ☐	26:47-64 ☐	26:65-75 ☐	27:1-26 ☐
12	27:27-44 ☐	27:45-56 ☐	27:57—28:15 ☐	28:16-20 ☐	Mark 1:1 ☐	1:2-6 ☐	1:7-13 ☐
13	1:14-28 ☐	1:29-45 ☐	2:1-12 ☐	2:13-28 ☐	3:1-19 ☐	3:20-35 ☐	4:1-25 ☐
14	4:26-41 ☐	5:1-20 ☐	5:21-43 ☐	6:1-29 ☐	6:30-56 ☐	7:1-23 ☐	7:24-37 ☐
15	8:1-26 ☐	8:27—9:1 ☐	9:2-29 ☐	9:30-50 ☐	10:1-16 ☐	10:17-34 ☐	10:35-52 ☐
16	11:1-16 ☐	11:17-33 ☐	12:1-27 ☐	12:28-44 ☐	13:1-13 ☐	13:14-37 ☐	14:1-26 ☐
17	14:27-52 ☐	14:53-72 ☐	15:1-15 ☐	15:16-47 ☐	16:1-8 ☐	16:9-20 ☐	Luke 1:1-4 ☐
18	1:5-25 ☐	1:26-46 ☐	1:47-56 ☐	1:57-80 ☐	2:1-8 ☐	2:9-20 ☐	2:21-39 ☐
19	2:40-52 ☐	3:1-20 ☐	3:21-38 ☐	4:1-13 ☐	4:14-30 ☐	4:31-44 ☐	5:1-26 ☐
20	5:27—6:16 ☐	6:17-38 ☐	6:39-49 ☐	7:1-17 ☐	7:18-23 ☐	7:24-35 ☐	7:36-50 ☐
21	8:1-15 ☐	8:16-25 ☐	8:26-39 ☐	8:40-56 ☐	9:1-17 ☐	9:18-26 ☐	9:27-36 ☐
22	9:37-50 ☐	9:51-62 ☐	10:1-11 ☐	10:12-24 ☐	10:25-37 ☐	10:38-42 ☐	11:1-13 ☐
23	11:14-26 ☐	11:27-36 ☐	11:37-54 ☐	12:1-12 ☐	12:13-21 ☐	12:22-34 ☐	12:35-48 ☐
24	12:49-59 ☐	13:1-9 ☐	13:10-17 ☐	13:18-30 ☐	13:31—14:6 ☐	14:7-14 ☐	14:15-24 ☐
25	14:25-35 ☐	15:1-10 ☐	15:11-21 ☐	15:22-32 ☐	16:1-13 ☐	16:14-22 ☐	16:23-31 ☐
26	17:1-19 ☐	17:20-37 ☐	18:1-14 ☐	18:15-30 ☐	18:31-43 ☐	19:1-10 ☐	19:11-27 ☐

Reading Schedule for the Recovery Version of the New Testament with Footnotes

Wk.	Lord's Day	Monday	Tuesday	Wednesday	Thursday	Friday	Saturday
27	Luke 19:28-48 ☐	20:1-19 ☐	20:20-38 ☐	20:39—21:4 ☐	21:5-27 ☐	21:28-38 ☐	22:1-20 ☐
28	22:21-38 ☐	22:39-54 ☐	22:55-71 ☐	23:1-43 ☐	23:44-56 ☐	24:1-12 ☐	24:13-35 ☐
29	24:36-53 ☐	John 1:1-13 ☐	1:14-18 ☐	1:19-34 ☐	1:35-51 ☐	2:1-11 ☐	2:12-22 ☐
30	2:23—3:13 ☐	3:14-21 ☐	3:22-36 ☐	4:1-14 ☐	4:15-26 ☐	4:27-42 ☐	4:43-54 ☐
31	5:1-16 ☐	5:17-30 ☐	5:31-47 ☐	6:1-15 ☐	6:16-31 ☐	6:32-51 ☐	6:52-71 ☐
32	7:1-9 ☐	7:10-24 ☐	7:25-36 ☐	7:37-52 ☐	7:53—8:11 ☐	8:12-27 ☐	8:28-44 ☐
33	8:45-59 ☐	9:1-13 ☐	9:14-34 ☐	9:35—10:9 ☐	10:10-30 ☐	10:31—11:4 ☐	11:5-22 ☐
34	11:23-40 ☐	11:41-57 ☐	12:1-11 ☐	12:12-24 ☐	12:25-36 ☐	12:37-50 ☐	13:1-11 ☐
35	13:12-30 ☐	13:31-38 ☐	14:1-6 ☐	14:7-20 ☐	14:21-31 ☐	15:1-11 ☐	15:12-27 ☐
36	16:1-15 ☐	16:16-33 ☐	17:1-5 ☐	17:6-13 ☐	17:14-24 ☐	17:25—18:11 ☐	18:12-27 ☐
37	18:28-40 ☐	19:1-16 ☐	19:17-30 ☐	19:31-42 ☐	20:1-13 ☐	20:14-18 ☐	20:19-22 ☐
38	20:23-31 ☐	21:1-14 ☐	21:15-22 ☐	21:23-25 ☐	Acts 1:1-8 ☐	1:9-14 ☐	1:15-26 ☐
39	2:1-13 ☐	2:14-21 ☐	2:22-36 ☐	2:37-41 ☐	2:42-47 ☐	3:1-18 ☐	3:19—4:22 ☐
40	4:23-37 ☐	5:1-16 ☐	5:17-32 ☐	5:33-42 ☐	6:1—7:1 ☐	7:2-29 ☐	7:30-60 ☐
41	8:1-13 ☐	8:14-25 ☐	8:26-40 ☐	9:1-19 ☐	9:20-43 ☐	10:1-16 ☐	10:17-33 ☐
42	10:34-48 ☐	11:1-18 ☐	11:19-30 ☐	12:1-25 ☐	13:1-12 ☐	13:13-43 ☐	13:44—14:5 ☐
43	14:6-28 ☐	15:1-12 ☐	15:13-34 ☐	15:35—16:5 ☐	16:6-18 ☐	16:19-40 ☐	17:1-18 ☐
44	17:19-34 ☐	18:1-17 ☐	18:18-28 ☐	19:1-20 ☐	19:21-41 ☐	20:1-12 ☐	20:13-38 ☐
45	21:1-14 ☐	21:15-26 ☐	21:27-40 ☐	22:1-21 ☐	22:22-29 ☐	22:30—23:11 ☐	23:12-15 ☐
46	23:16-30 ☐	23:31—24:21 ☐	24:22—25:5 ☐	25:6-27 ☐	26:1-13 ☐	26:14-32 ☐	27:1-26 ☐
47	27:27—28:10 ☐	28:11-22 ☐	28:23-31 ☐	Rom. 1:1-2 ☐	1:3-7 ☐	1:8-17 ☐	1:18-25 ☐
48	1:26—2:10 ☐	2:11-29 ☐	3:1-20 ☐	3:21-31 ☐	4:1-12 ☐	4:13-25 ☐	5:1-11 ☐
49	5:12-17 ☐	5:18—6:5 ☐	6:6-11 ☐	6:12-23 ☐	7:1-12 ☐	7:13-25 ☐	8:1-2 ☐
50	8:3-6 ☐	8:7-13 ☐	8:14-25 ☐	8:26-39 ☐	9:1-18 ☐	9:19—10:3 ☐	10:4-15 ☐
51	10:16—11:10 ☐	11:11-22 ☐	11:23-36 ☐	12:1-3 ☐	12:4-21 ☐	13:1-14 ☐	14:1-12 ☐
52	14:13-23 ☐	15:1-13 ☐	15:14-33 ☐	16:1-5 ☐	16:6-24 ☐	16:25-27 ☐	1 Cor. 1:1-4 ☐

Reading Schedule for the Recovery Version of the New Testament with Footnotes

Wk.	Lord's Day	Monday	Tuesday	Wednesday	Thursday	Friday	Saturday
53	1 Cor. 1:5-9 ☐	1:10-17 ☐	1:18-31 ☐	2:1-5 ☐	2:6-10 ☐	2:11-16 ☐	3:1-9 ☐
54	3:10-13 ☐	3:14-23 ☐	4:1-9 ☐	4:10-21 ☐	5:1-13 ☐	6:1-11 ☐	6:12-20 ☐
55	7:1-16 ☐	7:17-24 ☐	7:25-40 ☐	8:1-13 ☐	9:1-15 ☐	9:16-27 ☐	10:1-4 ☐
56	10:5-13 ☐	10:14-33 ☐	11:1-6 ☐	11:7-16 ☐	11:17-26 ☐	11:27-34 ☐	12:1-11 ☐
57	12:12-22 ☐	12:23-31 ☐	13:1-13 ☐	14:1-12 ☐	14:13-25 ☐	14:26-33 ☐	14:34-40 ☐
58	15:1-19 ☐	15:20-28 ☐	15:29-34 ☐	15:35-49 ☐	15:50-58 ☐	16:1-9 ☐	16:10-24 ☐
59	2 Cor. 1:1-4 ☐	1:5-14 ☐	1:15-22 ☐	1:23—2:11 ☐	2:12-17 ☐	3:1-6 ☐	3:7-11 ☐
60	3:12-18 ☐	4:1-6 ☐	4:7-12 ☐	4:13-18 ☐	5:1-8 ☐	5:9-15 ☐	5:16-21 ☐
61	6:1-13 ☐	6:14—7:4 ☐	7:5-16 ☐	8:1-15 ☐	8:16-24 ☐	9:1-15 ☐	10:1-6 ☐
62	10:7-18 ☐	11:1-15 ☐	11:16-33 ☐	12:1-10 ☐	12:11-21 ☐	13:1-10 ☐	13:11-14 ☐
63	Gal. 1:1-5 ☐	1:6-14 ☐	1:15-24 ☐	2:1-13 ☐	2:14-21 ☐	3:1-4 ☐	3:5-14 ☐
64	3:15-22 ☐	3:23-29 ☐	4:1-7 ☐	4:8-20 ☐	4:21-31 ☐	5:1-12 ☐	5:13-21 ☐
65	5:22-26 ☐	6:1-10 ☐	6:11-15 ☐	6:16-18 ☐	Eph. 1:1-3 ☐	1:4-6 ☐	1:7-10 ☐
66	1:11-14 ☐	1:15-18 ☐	1:19-23 ☐	2:1-5 ☐	2:6-10 ☐	2:11-14 ☐	2:15-18 ☐
67	2:19-22 ☐	3:1-7 ☐	3:8-13 ☐	3:14-18 ☐	3:19-21 ☐	4:1-4 ☐	4:5-10 ☐
68	4:11-16 ☐	4:17-24 ☐	4:25-32 ☐	5:1-10 ☐	5:11-21 ☐	5:22-26 ☐	5:27-33 ☐
69	6:1-9 ☐	6:10-14 ☐	6:15-18 ☐	6:19-24 ☐	Phil. 1:1-7 ☐	1:8-18 ☐	1:19-26 ☐
70	1:27—2:4 ☐	2:5-11 ☐	2:12-16 ☐	2:17-30 ☐	3:1-6 ☐	3:7-11 ☐	3:12-16 ☐
71	3:17-21 ☐	4:1-9 ☐	4:10-23 ☐	Col. 1:1-8 ☐	1:9-13 ☐	1:14-23 ☐	1:24-29 ☐
72	2:1-7 ☐	2:8-15 ☐	2:16-23 ☐	3:1-4 ☐	3:5-15 ☐	3:16-25 ☐	4:1-18 ☐
73	1 Thes. 1:1-3 ☐	1:4-10 ☐	2:1-12 ☐	2:13—3:5 ☐	3:6-13 ☐	4:1-10 ☐	4:11—5:11 ☐
74	5:12-28 ☐	2 Thes. 1:1-12 ☐	2:1-17 ☐	3:1-18 ☐	1 Tim. 1:1-2 ☐	1:3-4 ☐	1:5-14 ☐
75	1:15-20 ☐	2:1-7 ☐	2:8-15 ☐	3:1-13 ☐	3:14—4:5 ☐	4:6-16 ☐	5:1-25 ☐
76	6:1-10 ☐	6:11-21 ☐	2 Tim. 1:1-10 ☐	1:11-18 ☐	2:1-15 ☐	2:16-26 ☐	3:1-13 ☐
77	3:14—4:8 ☐	4:9-22 ☐	Titus 1:1-4 ☐	1:5-16 ☐	2:1-15 ☐	3:1-8 ☐	3:9-15 ☐
78	Philem. 1:1-11 ☐	1:12-25 ☐	Heb. 1:1-2 ☐	1:3-5 ☐	1:6-14 ☐	2:1-9 ☐	2:10-18 ☐

Reading Schedule for the Recovery Version of the New Testament with Footnotes

Wk.	Lord's Day	Monday	Tuesday	Wednesday	Thursday	Friday	Saturday
79	Heb. 3:1-6 ☐	3:7-19 ☐	4:1-9 ☐	4:10-13 ☐	4:14-16 ☐	5:1-10 ☐	5:11—6:3 ☐
80	6:4-8 ☐	6:9-20 ☐	7:1-10 ☐	7:11-28 ☐	8:1-6 ☐	8:7-13 ☐	9:1-4 ☐
81	9:5-14 ☐	9:15-28 ☐	10:1-18 ☐	10:19-28 ☐	10:29-39 ☐	11:1-6 ☐	11:7-19 ☐
82	11:20-31 ☐	11:32-40 ☐	12:1-2 ☐	12:3-13 ☐	12:14-17 ☐	12:18-26 ☐	12:27-29 ☐
83	13:1-7 ☐	13:8-12 ☐	13:13-15 ☐	13:16-25 ☐	James 1:1-8 ☐	1:9-18 ☐	1:19-27 ☐
84	2:1-13 ☐	2:14-26 ☐	3:1-18 ☐	4:1-10 ☐	4:11-17 ☐	5:1-12 ☐	5:13-20 ☐
85	1 Pet. 1:1-2 ☐	1:3-4 ☐	1:5 ☐	1:6-9 ☐	1:10-12 ☐	1:13-17 ☐	1:18-25 ☐
86	2:1-3 ☐	2:4-8 ☐	2:9-17 ☐	2:18-25 ☐	3:1-13 ☐	3:14-22 ☐	4:1-6 ☐
87	4:7-16 ☐	4:17-19 ☐	5:1-4 ☐	5:5-9 ☐	5:10-14 ☐	2 Pet. 1:1-2 ☐	1:3-4 ☐
88	1:5-8 ☐	1:9-11 ☐	1:12-18 ☐	1:19-21 ☐	2:1-3 ☐	2:4-11 ☐	2:12-22 ☐
89	3:1-6 ☐	3:7-9 ☐	3:10-12 ☐	3:13-15 ☐	3:16 ☐	3:17-18 ☐	1 John 1:1-2 ☐
90	1:3-4 ☐	1:5 ☐	1:6 ☐	1:7 ☐	1:8-10 ☐	2:1-2 ☐	2:3-11 ☐
91	2:12-14 ☐	2:15-19 ☐	2:20-23 ☐	2:24-27 ☐	2:28-29 ☐	3:1-5 ☐	3:6-10 ☐
92	3:11-18 ☐	3:19-24 ☐	4:1-6 ☐	4:7-11 ☐	4:12-15 ☐	4:16—5:3 ☐	5:4-13 ☐
93	5:14-17 ☐	5:18-21 ☐	2 John 1:1-3 ☐	1:4-9 ☐	1:10-13 ☐	3 John 1:1-6 ☐	1:7-14 ☐
94	Jude 1:1-4 ☐	1:5-10 ☐	1:11-19 ☐	1:20-25 ☐	Rev. 1:1-3 ☐	1:4-6 ☐	1:7-11 ☐
95	1:12-13 ☐	1:14-16 ☐	1:17-20 ☐	2:1-6 ☐	2:7 ☐	2:8-9 ☐	2:10-11 ☐
96	2:12-14 ☐	2:15-17 ☐	2:18-23 ☐	2:24-29 ☐	3:1-3 ☐	3:4-6 ☐	3:7-9 ☐
97	3:10-13 ☐	3:14-18 ☐	3:19-22 ☐	4:1-5 ☐	4:6-7 ☐	4:8-11 ☐	5:1-6 ☐
98	5:7-14 ☐	6:1-8 ☐	6:9-17 ☐	7:1-8 ☐	7:9-17 ☐	8:1-6 ☐	8:7-12 ☐
99	8:13—9:11 ☐	9:12-21 ☐	10:1-4 ☐	10:5-11 ☐	11:1-4 ☐	11:5-14 ☐	11:15-19 ☐
100	12:1-4 ☐	12:5-9 ☐	12:10-18 ☐	13:1-10 ☐	13:11-18 ☐	14:1-5 ☐	14:6-12 ☐
101	14:13-20 ☐	15:1-8 ☐	16:1-12 ☐	16:13-21 ☐	17:1-6 ☐	17:7-18 ☐	18:1-8 ☐
102	18:9—19:4 ☐	19:5-10 ☐	19:11-16 ☐	19:17-21 ☐	20:1-6 ☐	20:7-10 ☐	20:11-15 ☐
103	21:1 ☐	21:2 ☐	21:3-8 ☐	21:9-13 ☐	21:14-18 ☐	21:19-21 ☐	21:22-27 ☐
104	22:1 ☐	22:2 ☐	22:3-11 ☐	22:12-15 ☐	22:16-17 ☐	22:18-21 ☐	

Week 31 — Day 6 Today's verses

Matt. But I say to you that everyone who is an-
5:22 gry with his brother shall be liable to the
judgment...

Gen. There is no one greater in this house than
39:9 I, and he has withheld nothing from me
except you, because you are his wife.
How then can I do this great evil, and sin
against God?

12 ...[Joseph] left his garment in her hand,
and fled and went outside.

Date

Week 31 — Day 3 Today's verses

Gen. Then Joseph had a dream; and when he
37:5 told it to his brothers, they hated him even
more.

7 There we were, binding sheaves in the
field, when suddenly my sheaf rose up
and remained standing; and then your
sheaves gathered around and bowed
down to my sheaf.

Date

Week 31 — Day 5 Today's verses

Matt. And Judah begot Pharez and Zarah of
1:3 Tamar, and Pharez begot Hezron, and
Hezron begot Aram.

7:1 Do not judge, that you be not judged.

Date

Week 31 — Day 2 Today's verses

Gen. And Pharaoh was angry with his two
40:2-3 officials, the chief of the cupbearers and
the chief of the bakers. And he put them in
custody at the house of the captain of the
guard, in the prison, the place where
Joseph was confined.

Date

Week 31 — Day 4 Today's verses

Gen. And he had still another dream and told it
37:9 to his brothers and said, Now I have had
another dream: There were the sun and
the moon and eleven stars, bowing down
to me.

Rev. And a great sign was seen in heaven: a
12:1 woman clothed with the sun, and the
moon underneath her feet, and on her
head a crown of twelve stars.

Date

Week 31 — Day 1 Today's verses

Gen. ...Joseph, when he was seventeen years
37:2-4 old, was shepherding the flock with his
brothers while he was still a youth....Now
Israel loved Joseph more than all his sons
because he was the son of his old age,
and he had made him a coat of many
colors. And when his brothers saw that
their father loved him more than all his
brothers, they hated him and could not
speak peaceably to him.

Date

Week 32 — Day 4 — Today's verses

Gen. 41:42 ...Pharaoh took off his signet ring from his hand and put it upon Joseph's hand,... clothed him in garments of fine linen, and put a gold chain around his neck.

51-52 And Joseph called the name of the first-born Manasseh, for, *he said,* God has made me forget all my trouble and all my father's house. And he called the name of the second Ephraim, for, *he said,* God has made me fruitful in the land of my affliction.

_____
Date

Week 32 — Day 5 — Today's verses

Gen. 43:30-31 And Joseph hurried—for his inward parts burned for his brother—and sought a *place* to weep. So he entered into his chamber and wept there. Then he washed his face and came out, and he controlled himself and said, Serve the meal.

_____
Date

Week 32 — Day 6 — Today's verses

Gen. 47:18 ...When that year had ended, they came to him the second year and said to him, We cannot hide from my lord that our money has been spent, and the herds of cattle are my lord's. There is nothing left in the sight of my lord except our bodies and our lands.

23 Then Joseph said to the people, Now that I have this day bought you and your land for Pharaoh, here is seed for you that you may sow the land.

_____
Date

Week 32 — Day 1 — Today's verses

Gen. 41:40-41 You shall be over my household, and according to your word all my people shall be ruled; only in the throne will I be greater than you. Then Pharaoh said to Joseph, See, I have set you over all the land of Egypt.

_____
Date

Week 32 — Day 2 — Today's verses

Gen. 40:8 ...We have had a dream, and there is no one to interpret it. And Joseph said to them, Do not interpretations belong to God? Please tell *it* to me.

41:15-16 And Pharaoh said to Joseph, I have had a dream, but there is no one who can interpret it; and I have heard it said of you that when you hear a dream you can interpret it. And Joseph answered Pharaoh, saying, It is not of me; God will give Pharaoh a favorable answer.

_____
Date

Week 32 — Day 3 — Today's verses

Gen. 41:12-13 And a young Hebrew man was there with us, a servant of the captain of the guard. And we told him our dreams, and he interpreted them for us; to each one he interpreted according to his dream. And as he interpreted to us, so it happened; Pharaoh restored me to my office, and he hanged the baker.

_____
Date

Week 33 — Day 4	Today's verses
Num. 6:23-26	...Thus you shall bless the children of Israel; you shall say to them, Jehovah bless you and keep you; Jehovah make His face shine upon you and be gracious to you; Jehovah lift up His countenance upon you and give you peace.

Date

Week 33 — Day 5	Today's verses
2 Cor. 13:14	The grace of the Lord Jesus Christ and the love of God and the fellowship of the Holy Spirit be with you all.
Gen. 48:20	And he blessed them that day, saying, By you Israel will pronounce blessings, saying, God make you like Ephraim and like Manasseh. Thus he set Ephraim before Manasseh.

Date

Week 33 — Day 6	Today's verses
Gen. 48:14	But Israel stretched out his right hand and laid it upon Ephraim's head—although he was the younger—and his left hand upon Manasseh's head, guiding his hands with insight, even though Manasseh was the firstborn.
1 Cor. 7:40	But she is more blessed if she so remains, according to my opinion; but I think that I also have the Spirit of God.

Date

Week 33 — Day 1	Today's verses
Gen. 48:15-16	And he [Jacob] blessed Joseph and said, The God before whom my fathers Abraham and Isaac walked, the God who has shepherded me all my life to this day, the Angel who has redeemed me from all evil, bless the boys; and may my name be named on them, and the name of my fathers Abraham and Isaac; and may they be a teeming multitude in the midst of the earth.

Date

Week 33 — Day 2	Today's verses
Gen. 47:7	And Joseph brought in Jacob his father and set him before Pharaoh, and Jacob blessed Pharaoh.
Heb. 7:7	But without any dispute the lesser is blessed by the greater.
Gen. 48:9	And Joseph said to his father, They are my sons, whom God has given to me here. And he said, Bring them to me, please, that I may bless them.

Date

Week 33 — Day 3	Today's verses
Phil. 1:25	And being confident of this, I know that I will remain and continue with you all for your progress and joy of the faith.
Gen. 14:18-20	And Melchizedek the king of Salem brought out bread and wine. Now he was priest of God the Most High. And he blessed him and said, Blessed be Abram of God the Most High, Possessor of heaven and earth; and blessed be God the Most High...

Date

Week 34 — Day 4 Today's verses

Gen. The scepter will not depart from Judah,
49:10-12 nor the ruler's staff from between his feet,
until Shiloh comes, and to Him shall be
the obedience of the peoples. Binding his
foal to the vine, and his donkey's colt to
the choice vine, he washes his garment in
wine, and his robe in the blood of grapes.
Dark are his eyes with wine, and white
are his teeth with milk.

Date

Week 34 — Day 5 Today's verses

Gen. Zebulun will dwell at the shore of the sea,
49:13 and he will be a shore for ships, and his
flank will be toward Sidon.

Matt. "Land of Zebulun and land of Naphtali,
4:15 the way to the sea, beyond the Jordan,
Galilee of the Gentiles."

Deut. ...Rejoice, Zebulun, for your going forth...
33:18

Date

Week 34 — Day 6 Today's verses

Gen. Issachar is a strong donkey, couching be-
49:14-15 tween the sheepfolds. And he saw a resting place that was good and the land that
was pleasant, and he bowed his shoulder
to bear, and became a task-worker...

Deut. They shall call peoples to the mountain;
33:19 there they shall offer sacrifices of righteousness; for they shall suck the abundance of the seas and the hidden treasures of the sand.

Date

Week 34 — Day 1 Today's verses

Gen. Reuben, you are my firstborn, my might
49:3-4 and the firstfruits of my vigor, preeminent
in dignity and preeminent in power. Ebullient as water, you will not have the preeminence, because you went up to your
father's bed; then you defiled *it*—he went
up to my couch.

Deut. May Reuben live and not die, nor his men
33:6 be few.

Date

Week 34 — Day 2 Today's verses

Gen. Simeon and Levi are brothers; weapons of
49:5-7 violence are their swords. Come not into
their council, O my soul; be not united
with their assembly, O my glory; for in
their anger they slew men, and in their
self-will they hamstrung oxen. Cursed be
their anger, for it is fierce; and their wrath,
for it is cruel: I will divide them in Jacob,
and scatter them in Israel.

Date

Week 34 — Day 3 Today's verses

Gen. Judah, your brothers will praise you; your
49:8-9 hand will be on the neck of your enemies;
your father's sons will bow down before
you. Judah is a young lion; from the prey,
my son, you have gone up. He couches,
he stretches out like a lion, and like a lioness; who will rouse him up?

Rev. ...Do not weep; behold, the Lion of the
5:5 tribe of Judah, the Root of David, has
overcome...

Date

Week 35 — Day 4 Today's verses

Gen. 49:21 Naphtali is a hind let loose; he gives beautiful words.

Deut. 33:23 And concerning Naphtali he said, O Naphtali, satisfied with favor, and full of the blessing of Jehovah: possess the sea and the south.

_____
Date

Week 35 — Day 5 Today's verses

Gen. 49:22 Joseph is a fruitful bough, a fruitful bough by a fountain; *his* branches run over the wall.

25-26 ...From the All-sufficient One, who will bless you with blessings of heaven above, blessings of the deep that lies beneath, blessings of the breasts and of the womb. The blessings of your father surpass the blessings of my ancestors to the utmost bound of the everlasting hills...

_____
Date

Week 35 — Day 6 Today's verses

Gen. 49:27 Benjamin is a ravenous wolf, in the morning devouring the prey and in the evening dividing the spoil.

Deut. 33:12 Concerning Benjamin he said, The beloved of Jehovah shall dwell securely beside Him; *Jehovah* shall cover over him all the day, and He shall dwell between his shoulders.

_____
Date

Week 35 — Day 1 Today's verses

Gen. 49:16-18 Dan will judge his people, as one of the tribes of Israel. Dan will be a serpent in the way, a viper on the path, that bites the horse's heels, so that his rider falls backward. I have waited for Your salvation, O Jehovah.

Deut. 33:22 And concerning Dan he said, Dan is a lion's whelp that leaps forth from Bashan.

_____
Date

Week 35 — Day 2 Today's verses

Deut. 33:20-21 And concerning Gad he said, Blessed be He who enlarges Gad. He dwells as a lioness, and tears off the arm, yea, even the top of the head. And he provided the first part for himself, for there the portion of a lawgiver is reserved; and he came with the heads of the people; he executed the righteousness of Jehovah and His judgments with Israel.

_____
Date

Week 35 — Day 3 Today's verses

Gen. 49:20 Asher's food will be rich, and he will yield royal dainties.

Deut. 33:24-25 And concerning Asher he said, Blessed be Asher above the sons. May he be the one favored of his brothers, and the one dipping his foot in oil. Your doorbolts shall be iron and copper; and as your days are, so shall your strength be.

_____
Date

Week 36 — Day 4   Today's verses

Rom. Because those whom He foreknew, He
8:29 also predestinated to be conformed to the
image of His Son, that He might be the
Firstborn among many brothers.

5:17 For if, by the offense of the one, death
reigned through the one, much more
those who receive the abundance of
grace and of the gift of righteousness will
reign in life through the One, Jesus Christ.

Week 36 — Day 5   Today's verses

Col.   Who delivered us out of the authority of
1:13   darkness and transferred us into the kingdom of the Son of His love.

Eph.   And put on the new man, which was cre-
4:24   ated according to God in righteousness
and holiness of the reality.

Week 36 — Day 6   Today's verses

Matt. ...For Yours is the kingdom and the power
6:13   and the glory forever. Amen.

Rev.   Having the glory of God. Her light was
21:11 like a most precious stone, like a jasper
stone, as clear as crystal.

Week 36 — Day 1   Today's verses

Gen.   And God said, Let Us make man in Our
1:26   image, according to Our likeness; and let
them have dominion...over all the earth
and over every creeping thing that creeps
upon the earth.

28   And God blessed them; and God said to
them, Be fruitful and multiply, and fill the
earth and subdue it, and have dominion...

Week 36 — Day 2   Today's verses

Gen.   And Joseph brought in Jacob his father
47:7-8 and set him before Pharaoh, and Jacob
blessed Pharaoh. And Pharaoh said to
Jacob, How many are the years of your
life?

Psa.   The earth is Jehovah's, and its fullness, the
24:1   habitable land and those who dwell in it.

Week 36 — Day 3   Today's verses

Matt. From that time Jesus began to proclaim
4:17   and to say, Repent, for the kingdom of the
heavens has drawn near.

24:14 And this gospel of the kingdom will be
preached in the whole inhabited earth for
a testimony to all the nations, and then
the end will come.

Jacob - chosen, broken, dealt with, transformation - maturity - overflow of life - blessing others with Christ. The Lord crossing us out is the blessing - dying to self, dying to supplanting. The eternal blessing is what counts → May God bless a keep you (The Father) May His countenance shine upon you (The Son) and give you peace (The Spirit). The 3 fold blessing. To bless others - is to minister Christ to others. As a channel of Christ to others. Blessing is a matter of being in our spirit. As we exercise our spirit in all that we do we are a blessing a are blessing others - here and now. We do not need to get to maturity to be a blessing to others.